The Almond Tree Speaks
NEW & SELECTED WRITINGS
1974-1994

Murray Bodo, O.F.M.

ST. ANTHONY MESSENGER PRESS

CINCINNATI, OHIO

Cover and book design by Mary Alfieri
Illustrations by Mary Newell DePalma

ISBN 0-86716-237-6

copyright ©1994, Murray Bodo

All rights reserved.

Published by St. Anthony Messenger Press
Printed in the U.S.A.

I *said to the almond tree,*

"Sister, speak to me of God."

And the almond tree blossomed.

— Nikos Kazantzakis
Report to Greco

For my mother,

Polly Bodo,

1913-1989

San Francisco Peak outside Flagstaff
   the one we crossed back and forth
   between Winslow and Payson.
   I see it again against the moon,
   the sliding stars,
                 and your face
   turned from the departing train
   you couldn't see into
   but I could see out of,
   not knowing it would be
   the last time:
                 mountain
   dark against the waning moon.

Contents

Foreword

Even the modern adobe houses huddle close together like pueblos. People mass in one small spot as though around a fire, and all around them the immense expanse of sand and sagebrush, of mesas and dry arroyos. And over all an unearthly silence.

As a child I would sit for hours looking at the blankness as far as the eye could see, looking for something to focus on, some image to nourish my soul. But when they came, the images rose from within me, from my longing for something to fill the void, the silence. Usually they were images from the movies I watched every Saturday afternoon. I would see Hopalong Cassidy riding over the sandhill that stood watch across from our small adobe house on Fifth Street. Or Charley Chan would knock on the glassed-in porch that was my room and seek my advice on a particularly difficult case. Sometimes, when the wind howled or whined as it blew around the house or invaded my room through cracks and doorframes, angels or ghosts would enter, depending on whether I'd just seen something like *Joan of Arc* or listened to *The Whistler* on the radio.

And yet, for all these artificial images that flooded my mind, I continued to stare at the barren land hoping to see there something more interesting than the movies. It never happened, but something else did.

The brown and yellow grasses flattened by the wind, the distant mesas, the flat, unbroken horizon, all entered my soul and remain there today so many years after I left New Mexico and the Southwest for Ohio and, beyond that, for Italy and Greece, England and France.

I stand on a corner in Rome, waiting to risk crossing the chaos of cars, and a gust of wind suddenly transports me to a corner in downtown Gallup, usually Front Street, or Railroad Avenue, as it was once called, where the wind would catch me off guard, a small boy waiting to risk jumping across a freight train stopped at the First Street train crossing. Or on the Island of Mykonos I wake to sandhills that look, my back to the sea, like those around Zuni Pueblo, now transported to a Greek Island and painted white. And on the Island of Ischia I think I hear my father's voice calling my name from a passing fishing boat that seems the very one we fished from in Bluewater Lake when Dad returned from the war in the Pacific in 1946. Even in Assisi the New Mexico landscape rises up in the red tint of the soil, in the pink stones of the medieval houses, themselves pueblo-like in their piling and huddling for protection on the side of Mount Subasio.

Someone once said that every landscape we love is the geography of our own soul. Somehow, then, my soul must have sagebrush in it, and dry sand blowing, and lonely steers, and sheep with starved-looking dogs dragging their weary bodies round and round the sheep, their eyes wary and bloodshot for coyotes and bear. And illuminating everything, the dazzling, relentless sun, replaced at night by stars whose brilliance I've seen nowhere else, except perhaps in Greece.

Out of and on this landscape within are the characters of my imagination—Saint Francis, Saint Clare, Brother Juniper, Jesus. They all walk toward me out of the New Mexico desert.

And for over twenty years I've been trying to find words to render those desert images on the page. The first image began when I was thirteen years old sitting outside reading a life of Saint Francis of Assisi. The image that began there found its

words twenty-two years later in 1972 with the writing of
Francis: The Journey and the Dream. The writing of that book
freed other images, and book followed book, from *Walk in
Beauty* in 1974 to the present volume in 1994: *Song of the
Sparrow* (1976), *Clare, A Light in the Garden* (1979), *Sing
Pilgrimage and Exile* (1980), *Letters From Pleasant Street* (1981),
Juniper, Friend of Francis, Fool of God (1983), *The Way of St.
Francis* (1984), *Jesus, A Disciple's Search* (1986), *Through the
Year With Francis of Assisi* (1987), *Tales of St. Francis* (1988),
Clare, A Light in the Garden: Revised and Expanded (1992).

So, when the editors of St. Anthony Messenger Press asked me
for a book that would represent my writing over the past
twenty years, I turned again to the desert in search of images.
And there, like an old almond tree on a barren hillside, were
the same images, some healthy, some drying up like an almond
nut at the end of a withering branch. I searched the tree for
what I thought were still healthy branches.

This was hard to do at first, because I wanted all the previous
writing to be healthy. But I would have to choose because of
the limitations of space. Thus began a pruning process whose
purpose was new life, renewed vigor. The still healthy branches
I then grafted onto a new plant and let them grow together. My
hope is that this grafting has produced a healthy new tree, an
almond tree that will speak anew of God.

On Amtrak's *Southwest Chief*
Between Isleta and Laguna
Summer 1993

❖

From
Sing Pilgrimage and Exile
(1980)

❖

Views From My Window

A soft rain falls outside my window and the maple tree across
the drive looks, for all its golden beauty, forlorn and ready to
lose the last of its leaves. I think it was raining the day I
discovered you, Francis. At least it was autumn and a driving
wind forced me into the school library to escape the
melancholy sound of fall. I can still see the little book standing
on the shelf, and the little flowers around the edges; but I don't
remember who wrote it or what the title was. I think it was
simply *Francis of Assisi*. I have often thought of going back to
that little room and trying to recreate that discovery just as it
was so long ago. But the school has burned to the ground now,
and all the books with it. And perhaps that is good for me, the
burning of attachments and mementos, even of you, Father
Francis.

It was there in that little public school library that I realized
not so much your joy, Francis, as my own emptiness and lack of
everything you possessed in having nothing. There it began,
the void, the nothingness which had to be filled and which
only your challenge could fill. I saw in you a way to peace and
joy, and that way was Christ in his poverty, Christ in his
emptying.

The rest is history now. Leaving home at fourteen, the long
journey from New Mexico to Ohio, the years of study, the
habit, the vows, ordination. Only—through it all and even
now, you still haunt me, Francis. Sometimes I see your face
behind the glass of department stores and around corners,
watching me, calling me out toward you, and toward some

goal, some dream I haven't yet caught. You, always you, like some phantom of my own dreaming, suddenly flashing across my mind—a shadow of that face I met reading a book in the corner of a library when I was thirteen years old.

II.

The rain outside has turned to snow. What are you saying now, Father, in the coldness of that November sign of winter coming once again? It is a wet snow with nothing sticking to the ground, but the sky has become almost black to match the blackness of tree trunks across the landscape. And in this austere and damp afternoon your face again appears, Francis, laced with the slender black branches of winter's early coming. And the winter of your life is etched firmly in my mind—those black days when what you tried so hard to achieve among the brothers seemed threatened by practicalities and growing numbers, by Church laws and mediocrity and a loss of the original vision. And the darkness of winter fell upon the bright Camelot of the beginning when you and Leo and Masseo and the others charged about the countryside proclaiming your knighthood, unafraid and filled with love.

III.

Often when I look out my second-floor window in the late fall, I think of you in your sickness before the great dawn of your conversion. I think of the late, late days of your life when autumn fell from the mountains and threatened to plunge you once again into the despair of those long days when you lay in bed puffing out your lips, exhausting the spirit of all your young days on empty walls. And the low-hanging clouds seem to

3

settle heavily on the green woods and the black branches of leafless trees, like all the threats upon the brotherhood.

IV.

Winter is settling down on my small room now. A soft mist is alternating from snow to drizzle. The trees are taking on that black, charcoal color that is a part of my memories of this same seminary when I was a boy of fourteen. On days like this I would snuggle up in a corner of the library with a good book and hope that all the bright fluorescent lights of the world would keep out the darkness I feared. But today, Francis, so many years after, I walk out in our woods on a day like this. Somewhere along those years with you my quest drove me inward toward that darkness I so feared. And in the encounter there, at the core of my own fear, I broke through something to a new and hitherto hidden center of my heart where all was light and hope, where I found a small warm flame to keep me from the cold and dark and where I knew I could flee if necessary. But always in my journeys back to that small but infinite space within, I have to pass through the dark of which this day reminds me. And always it is frightening and panic-filled because of the gnawing suspicion that the flame will not be there. Perhaps that is what you felt during those long days in the cave outside Assisi when you feared the light of day and scurried off to hide in a deep cavern where any light at all had to come from within your own heart. And you persevered, didn't you, until you were sure that the flame was real?

4

V.

The view from my window this morning is one of those bright winter days when everything stands out in sharp detail, when the blue of the sky brightens the bare black trees and coats their sun sides with a silver sheen. The contrast of black and silver against the blue backdrop reminds me again of your Lady Poverty. It was she who shone so brightly on the austere deprivation of your life and by some strange alchemy turned to silver the crude ore you extracted from the bowels of your world. Those black trees that looked so ominous when the rain was falling outside my window are now transparent with that radiance which is the gift of a day like this. And that glory does not come from within but is projected from the sun through blue sky like a fine white sand transforming but not obliterating the somber landscape of my window world. I would not have noticed the silver out there were it not for the stark black trees that first affronted me when all the leaves were gone.

You fought so hard, Francis, for your Lady Poverty, knowing that only she would bring luster to the plainness of your brotherhood. As long as her countenance shone on the brotherhood, they would take something of her bright light and reflect it, mirroring her beauty to the world.

VI.

This rainy morning's darkness that grows darker as the sun rises invisibly behind the unbroken layers of wet clouds reminds me again, Francis, of the need for light. How very much of joy and love is cut off from us when we let the darkness outside overcome the light that burns within our hearts. The lights of

the cars that dully burn past my window in this morning
darkness make no impression on the gray that is not night.
Something more than candle power is needed to light the way
for the listless eyes of morning commuters.

VII.

Something in that white birch's swaying makes this morning's
view new for me. I had never really looked far enough toward
the sun's rising to see it. And yet like you, Francis, it has always
been there behind that little lip of windowsill I never bothered
to look around. Even though the view from my window is
already limited and confined to the span of my own horizon, I
find myself drawing together even more compactly what I want
to see. And soon I'm looking only at what I expect to see when
I roll up my shades in the morning. Certain features in the
landscape I single out and emphasize—as I do with your life
and Rule. It wasn't till I moved to another floor and looked
outside from another angle that I saw a birch tree trembling in
the wind. From what new height and angle should I now view
you, Father Francis? Perhaps in that ragged little sparrow
swaying in the birch tree I will catch on wing some fleeting
glimpse of the Little Poor Man, the poet and mystic, the saint
that you are.

Childhood Memories

Every little boy should have a grandfather. When I was a little
boy, I had a grandfather who wasn't really a grandfather;
anyway that's what everybody said. But I knew he was my
grandfather, even though my parents didn't know him, and he
lived on the other side of the tracks and he was a Navajo.
Everyone called him Medicine Man and that always brought to
my seven-year-old mind rows and rows of aspirin bottles that I
imagined he gave to all the sick people in the world.

I first met my grandfather at the Santa Fe train station in
Gallup. He had long gun-gray hair which he kept tied up in a
neat little ball on the back of his head, and he sold turquoise
rings to tourists who stopped at the Fred Harvey House to
stretch their legs whenever the *El Capitan* or the *Chief* or *Grand
Canyon Limited* stopped in Gallup. Grandfather was always
there, his rings spread out on a Navajo rug, his back propped
against the beige stucco wall of the depot.

My mother worked all day in the laundry behind the depot and
my daddy worked all day on an island in the South Pacific. He
was a marine sergeant and wore long shiny medals for
marksmanship. My grandfather was my daytime companion
and friend and I sat for long hours after school, when the other
kids were playing, and talked with my grandfather, the
medicine man.

It was always warm sitting on the rug next to my grandfather.
He would tell me about Corn Woman and Pollen Boy and
Bluebird and how the Navajos, whom he always called Dineh,

the people, came out of the belly of the earth. My whole childhood was filled with stories and pictures, the odor of raw blanket wool and the low quiet tones of my grandfather's voice.

II.

I take up my pen,
and I remember.
I reach down deep inside
for the feel of things
the way they were.
I smell again the sagebrush,
and I taste the piñon,
and I hear the trains
coughing into Gallup.
A small boy, five years old,
is holding a Daisy B-B gun.
He is standing by a little brick house
on Aztec Avenue.
It is December 7, 1941.
The war begins.

III.

Trains rumble through my childhood
squealing and steaming and grunting up
speed, their melancholy groans sooting
my world with ashes of now.
I used to stand on the Harvey House
platform looking before and after,
longing to jump onto a train

and watch the coal dust blow
behind me as I stood in the engine
cab, arm on the window, my right
hand jerking squirts of whistle
before me, clearing the tracks,
heralding eternal comings and goings,
leaving ashes settling forever
on the concrete slabs of passing
railroad platforms.

IV.

There was a boy's sip of apricot brandy in the back seat as we
drove back from rabbit hunting. It wasn't always snowing, but
there was always snow on the ground, and you were glad you
had on thick woolen socks and leather boots with plenty of
neat's-foot oil rubbed into them. Rabbits were plentiful then.
You didn't get that awful, sorry feeling you get now when you
spot one lonely rabbit shivering inside a clump of sage, waiting
for your finger on the trigger. It was more like you were doing
nature a favor by thinning out the rabbits and bringing home
scores of cottontails that would keep the family going all
winter if they were dressed right and put down in the freezer in
good packing.

Usually, we went to San Mateo for our rabbits because that's
where they were. Anyway, that's what Dad said, and I never
doubted him when it came to hunting.

V.

Empty balloon,
inner tube discarded
in a corner of the room
where we worked, half-hearted,
on Saturday mornings to earn
enough for the movies in the afternoon.
Still in the corner, still helpless for air
poor inner tube, flattened balloon,
I never noticed you back there
when I was a boy of June.
I see you now and
scream for air.

VI.

I remember the last tune
I danced. I was thirteen
and the dance was a farewell
for me and I danced with
the mother of my childhood sweetheart
who never knew she was my girl.
And then the dance was over
until now. I remember, and
I want to dance again. I
realize I am nearing forty.
No trauma, really. I just want
to dance. In more ways than one
I want to dance—to make up
for something, to be going again.
So I run to the altar with a tan.

VII.

When, in the windswept childhood
of my desert days, I saw my heart,
etched on the sandhills, blowing away,
I did what I could to befriend the wind.
And now, when the sound of the wind
beckons me, I return to sandhills
to see how much of my heart remains
outlined on the face of the red rocks
standing sentinel at the edge of town.

❖

From
Walk in Beauty
(1974)

❖

You take State Route 666 and travel north from Gallup, and it isn't long before you realize how desolate the land really is. The silence of sagebrush and sand begins almost immediately, and you are transported into an ageless desert that seems unconcerned and untroubled by highways bulging with cars, pickup trucks and semi-trailers, and big jet planes so high in the New Mexico sky that a thin line of white smoke is their only mark. This country is the beginning of Navajoland, a country as vast and mysterious as the legends and myths of its origins.

It is a land that cast its spell on me the very first time I traveled through it as a small boy. I've crossed it and lived on it many times since. I've left this country for long periods in my life, but always I return, return to the mystic sound of its silence, to the space that opened my imagination, to the people, the Navajos who move always on the endless trails that wind through my mind.

Sunrise on the reservation. The morning air is fresh and you feel the beginning of things. There is something mystic about looking east, something related to the sun, to resurrection, to the cycle of rebirth following death and darkness upon the land. That hope of rising, that share in the sun's journey, all peoples tell somewhere in their mythologies, and they believe it or want to believe it in their deep hearts' yearning.

It is early morning. I am walking a sand bed that once was the bottom of a great inland sea. I stop and listen to the seagulls and surf far above me, and I understand that dimension of prayer which is a thirst and a pleading for water. Flash floods visit this desert flat from time to time like those moments of inspiration, those visitations of the spirit that vanish as suddenly as they come, leaving the ground dry again thirsting for the sea that once was everywhere.

Desert flower. Your round mystery draws me down into your soft, deep center. My entry there must be gentle, delicate, or I will shatter some symmetry of the universe. The Navajo Way to you is reverence, the Francis Way is poverty of spirit. Both Ways release you to the desert air and do not violate your secret.

The music of the desert. What is its tune, what is its rhythm? It sings in your ears long after you've gone to the hills and cities beyond. It rings in your brain and you only hear it there from time to time when you are alone and when you are quiet enough inside to remember that peace, as fragile as tiny grains of sand, which the smallest wind can lift and blow away.

I am alone here, and the smell of the rain on the red sand has an edge of sage in it. The breeze during a rain freshens the heart and the edge of sage is pleasantly wet. Everything will be dry again a few minutes afterward as if the rain itself were a mirage. I don't know anywhere else this happens except in the desert. There is no lingering sweetness in the air, only a dry heat rising from the ground. And you learn to enjoy the rain while it is falling.

On the floor of this canyon, looking up and out into the clear blue sky, I remember Saint Francis and the contemplative side of his nature. All the elements of his longing are here. The silence, the heightened awareness of nature, the poverty of simple folk, the sheep which always reminded him of the Lamb of God, and these sheer canyon walls which, like a mountaintop, lift your eyes toward heaven. Prayer is easy here and you feel almost guilty for this gift of escape, except that canyons are not for living in. You visit them from time to time and you wish you could stay. But you do not. You leave and you remember. And in that sense only, canyons are forever.

If you care about silence and listening to the dawn, you will rise at 4:30 or 5:00 and go to the sand dunes when night is still in the air and the blue light of morning burns on the horizon. There, before the birds begin to sing, before the dogs bark awake the sheep and horses, you can hear your own heart and mind clearly and prayer rises easily from the hushed and holy hills of this desert sanctuary. And in this breathless interval before the sun, God visits the earth.

❖

Out here the wind blows. Little funnels of wind and sand skitter over the desert, and often in March and April huge sandstorms settle in. A dark, impenetrable cloud seizes the land and whips it into a tempest and you don't even think of going outside until the storm has vented itself. It is when the storm is on you that you ask why the Dineh, the Navajos, continue to live on this dry, barren land.

In the world of sand there are skeletons, skulls mostly, but
sometimes whole carcasses lying white and naked in the sun.
The sand blows through them and around them, covering
them and uncovering them, polishing them like finished
sculptures. Coming upon them in the bright noonday sun, you
are surprised by death staring at you from an eyeless socket. But
these stark forms are strangely beautiful and death itself loses
its terror in your familiarity with this desert gallery of polished
bone.

What of sheep? Why do their bells ring through my mind
whenever I think of New Mexico and Arizona? Is it only
because they are really there, or is there a connection to
something deeper? There is a rhythm in sheep bells, a rhythm
that washes the mind, a rhythm of the soul like the lapping of
waves on the beach. And you hear the rhythm and it
transcends the sound of bells. It enters the mind and heart and
you are in another time, another simpler, more primitive
existence. The Navajos live there and you who live with them
share dimly, mysteriously in their consciousness of some
emergence, some beginning we all have in common. Sheep are
the memory of symbols that link past and present, tribe and
tribe—and the tribes of Israel and Changing Woman.[1]

❖

From the Lukachukai Mountains you can see the land. The
desert stretches below you on all four sides and to the north
Shiprock stands at anchor in the still brown sea. When I was a
boy, my father and his fishing buddies and I would speed past

Shiprock almost every weekend on our way to the cool Colorado trout streams. I had never seen the ocean or a sailing vessel, so Shiprock became my frigate on the high seas and I would fire a volley past her bow from the back seat of our Chevy while my father and his friends talked of fishing.

When we returned to Gallup every Sunday night, I would wait excitedly for Shiprock to come into view once again. I would adjust my spyglass and scan the emptiness for her. And then she would suddenly emerge like a submarine surfacing on the horizon. I would prepare the men for the attack and caution them to wait until we were as close as possible before we commenced firing. It was great fun always, and Shiprock became my private pirate ship on countless voyages across dry, waveless seas of sand.

Today it is still there and I spy it again from the Lukachukai Mountains. There are little specks down there on the dry ocean floor. Navajo, trader and tourist all look alike from this height. The Navajos say these mountains are holy.

In the mountains the air is clean and you don't feel that grit of sand on your teeth that is always there on the desert floor. Your whole being is lifted with the mountains and you understand why the Navajos call them sacred and why the psalmist cries, "I lift up my eyes toward the hills," and why Saint Francis built hermitages on the mountaintops.

The vertical loom, the yarn, the fork, the batten are all she needs. Then sitting in lotus position before the loom, with no pattern but the one in her mind, she weaves. The Navajo woman weaving. The artist before the altar of her offering. The loom and the woman, like madonna and child, are a unity of the creative spirit deep in the Navajo soul. Row upon row she deftly places the wefts, and her attention to each stripe, like any true artist's attention to detail, makes her rug a thing of beauty, an extension in wool of her unique creative gift.

Time is not wearing a wristwatch, not owning a phone. It is having no measuring instrument but the sun. It is not being controlled by a mechanical device which tells you that you should be somewhere or go somewhere or do something. Time is a rhythm to life, not a ticking that quickens the nerves. Time is sacred; it is walking with the sun. Time is a gift of tranquility from the Navajos.

Silence and space, and in March, sandstorms that rip you off the face of the earth. The quiet of the desert, and the ferocity of wind rearranging the landscape. Land of contrasts and surprises. That is the Arizona which greeted the first Franciscan missionaries on October 7, 1898.

I see them making the long journey by train from Cincinnati to Gallup, and then by wagon the last thirty miles to Cienega Ranch just across the northeastern border of Arizona. None of them has ever been West before, and it is like landing on a strange new planet, a planet barren of the grass and flowers they were used to in Cincinnati.

The three friars sit silently huddled together wondering how in the world they ended up here. And they resign themselves to the land and to its silent moods.

Three come at first, then more, and more, until the *Ednishodi* (those who drag their gowns) are an integral part of Navajoland, as endemic to the desert and hills of the Southwest as the sandhills are. They come imbued with the ideals of Francis of Assisi, with his littleness and his poverty of spirit. They come with their hands and hearts and minds committed to advancing the Kingdom of God on earth. They succeed seldom, they fail often, but they persevere as only men who love can. They ask nothing for themselves except the privilege of serving God and their beloved Dineh, the noble people who are the Navajo, proud nation of warriors and silversmiths, of rug-weavers and sheepherders; the Navajos, myth makers and artists, quiet sages of the mysteries of their sacred mountains and plains.

Yellow Meadow: Cienega Amarilla. It lies out there on the desert surrounded by tall sandstone sculptures that stand watch over the Reservation like silent prehistoric sentinels.

They come and set up a mission there next to the beautiful meadow. And they stay. And the mission grows.

They build a school there, of sandstone and mortar. And it also grows.

Like the Navajo hogan, St. Michaels chapel faces the dawn. To the south of the mission lies Cienega Amarilla, the yellow meadow, which gave its name to the original ranch that lay in this small valley. There is water in the meadow and I am reminded of the living waters in a dry land, a symbol of what the friars hope to bring to the Navajos. They dream of the living waters of Christ flooding from the south portal of the mission, but they know that time alone will tell if the Navajos can or will in fact drink of these waters. To the west and north lie the mountains and the depths of the Navajo myths and mysteries, and the Navajos may never come to Cienega Amarilla. In the waiting the friars grow humble and wise and the waters continue to flow and are there for the asking.

The chapel of St. Michaels Mission. It contains mysteries of my childhood held darkly in the corners of its pine and sandstone odors. When I was a boy, a journey to St. Michaels was an odyssey as grand and expansive as all of Homer, even though it was but thirty miles from Gallup. And the chapel itself was my Ithaca.

The melancholy whine of the wind through the dark painted glass windows of St. Michaels chapel. The bowed head of the crucified Christ outside that faces the chapel doors. This should be a depressing place to pray, but it is not and I wonder why it is so. The sound of the wind is comforting and the creak of the wooden doors somehow draws me to this place. There is solitude here without loneliness. Perhaps it is something in the wind.

The bell of St. Michaels Mission has a dull sound, as if it only reluctantly announces Mass in the beautiful meadow, as if it is hesitant to disturb the sheep quietly eating the sparse grass, as if it were a superimposition on the quieter bells of the Navajo ceremonials.

The zeal of the Christian missionary has not always been accompanied by knowledge of or reverence for the religion and myths of the peoples to whom the gospel message is preached. And like the bell of St. Michaels Mission the sound of the "Good News" can be an unwelcome intrusion, disturbing the tranquility and peace of a land steeped in tradition, a land as sacred to the Navajo as the Holy Land was and is to the Jew and the Christian.

The first Franciscan missionaries to come to Arizona understood this fundamental fact.

Father Berard Haile, who came to St. Michaels in 1900, once said, "I hope the time is far off when I must preach to these Indians and that for courtesy or some other reason they would willy-nilly listen to me.... Such a policy...of forcing doctrines upon the people against their desires, against their protests...is against my grain."

Across the road from the present mission, with a lone cedar tree in front of it, stands the original stone house that served as the first mission of the friars. Except for a butane gas tank in front of the house and electric wires outside, it looks pretty much the same. But this stone house looks more alone in the old photographs of it. There is a huge cross erected outside with the friars standing seemingly forlorn beneath it. There is no corpus on the cross, as if Christ himself had abandoned them, and they stand stiffly, waiting for him to reappear around a curve in the road. You feel, somehow, that they have been told not to run, not to follow after, but to wait and watch for someone.

There is no cross there anymore and the first friars are gone and the new mission buzzes with people and activity. The house alone remains and it is now a museum of all that was. There the rooms and mementos and early photographs tell the loneliness and anxiety of beginnings.

The way of the *Ednishodi*, the way of Francis, the little poor man, is the way of praise. This is what they say to the Navajo, this is the word the *Ednishodi* bring with them:

Praised be you, my Lord, in all your
Creatures, especially Sir Brother Sun,
Who makes the day and enlightens us through you.
He is lovely and radiant and grand;
And he heralds You, his most high Lord.
Praised be you, my Lord, for Sister Moon
And for the stars.
You have hung them in the heaven shining and precious
    and fair.
And praise to you, my Lord, in Brother Wind,
In air and cloud, calm, and every weather
That sustains your creatures.
Praised be You, my Lord, for Sister Water,
So very useful, humble, precious, and chaste.

Yes, and praise to you, my Lord, for Brother Fire.
Through him you illumine our night,
And he is handsome and merry, robust and strong.
Praised be you, my Lord, for our sister, Mother Earth,
Who nourishes us and teaches us,
Bringing forth all kinds of fruits and colored flowers and herbs.

The way of the Navajo, the Blessingway, is the way of
harmony. And this is what they say to the *Ednishodi*, this is
how they answer:

Now I was surrounded by Sun's surroundings,
when with the aid of a beautiful one I walked about.
Now I am long life, now happiness....
Behind me blessing is extended to mountains
Before me blessing is extended to mountains
Below me blessing is extended to the earth
Above me blessing is extended to the sky
At dawn I walk.
Behind me it is blessed where I walk, before me it is blessed
where I walk,
I walk, at dawn I walk.[2]

The gospel, the Good News. Blessingway, the Way of
Harmony. Two ways to God, two ways from God to humanity.
Do they fork in the road and wind ever in opposite directions,
or are they like forks in the desert that seem to cross each other
over and over again binding together the vast, lonely land?

The Navajo Reservation. Why does it grow on the missionary? Silence, space, timelessness, a way of life that still revolves with the seasons and with the weather.

An invisible shield protecting you from what is vulgar and cheap and dehumanizing in the space age. The space is not out there among the stars; it is all around you and within you.

You leave St. Michaels and drive west for about ten minutes and you are on a mountain summit where it is cool and quiet in the summer and the wind in the pines calms your troubled spirit. You sit beneath these pines and listen. How many friars must have come here down the years. How many disappointments and frustrations must have blown away with this wind in the pines. How many problems were clarified on this mountain. Out here you can always flee to the mountains, and Anglo and Navajo are one in what they seek and find in the pines.

In the early morning when a touch of the night-chill is still in the air, I walk the garden of St. Michaels School. It is quiet here, like the old monastery gardens on the California coast. There are trees in the garden and grass and little attempts at flowers, and I am aware of the time and patience and care it took to fashion this small oasis in the desert. It is a careful corner of the East transplanted here, a remembrance of what they left behind who came to Cienega, a pledge of what they hope to achieve, a symbol of what they have already done. These Sisters of the Blessed Sacrament, like the Franciscan

Sisters of Mary who run the dispensary and school for children who are mentally and physically handicapped, bring a touch of grace to the land. They both have gardens and they are women, virgins, flowering in a dry land.

This is really, in a sense, a book of memories, my own and those of others who remember the early Franciscans. It is as accurate and as selective as memory itself. We remember what is significant to us, for whatever reason, and we forget what is not important to us. My most vivid memory of St. Michaels, for example, is slippered old Father Berard Haile, standing in the basement next to the printing press, talking to a fourteen-year-old seminarian through a huge cloud of cigar smoke. All of those details are important to me, and are, twenty-two years later, symbolic of everything he was. My memory has jettisoned everything else about that meeting, except Father Berard's reply to my question, "Are you the priest who made Navajo into a written language?"

"Well, I was around during those years."

---

[1] "...Changing Woman is held in universal esteem by the Navaho.... The creation of the various...people on the earth is attributed to [her], and took place at her dwelling in the West. The Navaho...clans were created from parts of her body." *An Ethnologic Dictionary of the Navaho Language* (St. Michaels, Arizona: The Franciscan Fathers, 1910), pp. 355-356.

[2] By permission from *Blessing Way: With Three Versions of the Myth Recorded and Translated From the Navajo,* by Father Berard Haile, O.F.M., Leland C. Wyman (Tucson: University of Arizona Press, 1970).

From
Letters From Pleasant Street
(1981)

Poverty

I am living now in a section of Cincinnati called Over-the-Rhine. There are six of us here, Franciscans in a small friary on Pleasant Street. It is pleasant here, pleasant to be living in a small house, pleasant to be doing little domestic things like cooking and cleaning, pleasant to have neighbors and to wake up to the small sounds of a home coming to life.

Our neighbors are white Southern Appalachians and Blacks. On Pleasant Street they talk to one another and live side-by-side reasonably well. All of them are poor, and they worry about the price of everything. Yesterday at the A&P I watched an old black woman carry a bag of potatoes to the cashier as carefully as you would a piece of Waterford crystal. She waited until the cashier weighed it and announced, "One dollar fifty-seven, honey."

"Oh, my goodness. Guess you'll have to take out a few."

She could afford only a dollar's worth. And the clerk was kind as she gently removed the extra potatoes.

I stood behind the old woman with a $5.77-can of coffee in my hand, and suddenly I held it more carefully, reverently, for it had become almost six purchases of potatoes, an old woman's dream. And now coffee in the morning is precious to me. I realize how dear the sum $5.77 really is.

Then there's the old man across the street who sits on his stoop and greets me with a smile and a few words every day as I walk to the parking lot beside his house. He lights up as I walk by decked out in nice, bright clothes, bound for a world he will never enter. He doesn't have a car in the lot as we do, but I see no condemnation in his eyes. Rather, he is happy simply watching and admiring the parade passing in front of his house.

I look forward to seeing him and the man upstairs who leans out his window and teases about the furious pipe smoke that is always swirling about my head. I dress well every day for these men. I try to have my pipe lit when I stop to talk to them, and I carry them with me wherever I go. It makes all my goings bright because I feel somehow sent by them.

Around the corner from us is a little bar with a sign in the window, "Where friendly people meet." I've never been inside this café, but every time I pass by, I look in. There's a lot of pain in there, the hard side of poverty, of despair. When I look in, faces down the whole length of the bar are turned out looking at me. They are the faces of those who drink early in the morning. Trembling hands clutch the cool glasses, but they don't look at their drinks, these men and women. They drink and look outside. They drink and turn away to watch me walk by from my comfortable apartment, in my comfortable clothes, my mind set on passing them by.

The two old men with smiles and these faces are my new world. I feel compelled to enter that bar, to sit on the steps with my two friends and talk. I feel small, unworthy to enter their lives and more unworthy still to try to write it all down. That is my poverty, my emptiness. Perhaps if I could tell their stories, I could share their joy, their pain. Perhaps I never can.

Living Simply

A fine October rain is falling, streaking my windows, emphasizing the verticals of this inner-city world. Framed in the foreground of my long, narrow window are the black fire escapes that cling like playground monkey bars to our red brick apartment, and behind them the tower of old St. John's Church, balancing the slender chimney of the apartment across the street from us. One of Cincinnati's seven hills climbs behind the spire of St. John's. Nothing visually restful in all these straight, vertical lines, and yet I am relaxed here.

This past week a friend and I took the time to refinish an old oak dresser for my room. I had never worked with wood before, and never felt the grain beneath my fingertips grow smooth from patient sanding and the working-in of linseed oil. I didn't feel rushed refinishing this lovely piece of furniture. We worked in an atmosphere of leisure, and our long horizontal strokes with the grain smoothed something rough within us.

I love this dresser in my little third-floor garret because it represents what I am trying to do here: to reclaim the leisure that years of busyness have lost for me. I know I've always had time to refinish an old piece of furniture before, but I never did because I always had furniture in my room and because I never had the leisure, though I had the time.

I see now that having time for something and having leisure are two different things. Though I had time before, I had no leisure because the time between activities was filled with preoccupation about what I had just completed and with worry about the next task to be fulfilled. If the time between doings is too short, time doing nothing is as intense an activity as working, and there is not that tranquility of soul that is leisure.

Creative leisure is something inside, in the soul, and it can only happen when I am free enough to waste time, to play. Refinishing a piece of furniture is really play. You lose yourself exploring and discovering with a child's curiosity the possibilities and the mystery of wood. You are reclaiming something of your youth, of that period before adolescence when time was for you instead of against you.

Leisure is an attitude of the soul that allows time to be positive and creative again. To reach that point of leisure in our lives we have to cast out some demons: guilt and fear of being useless and the conviction that our self-worth is tied up with doing good. Time is not positive or creative; time is neutral. It is we who make time what it is. Only we can make that fundamental decision to be quiet and listen and surrender to play.

My dresser is finished now, and it stands as a reminder that leisure produces something more beautiful than does busy work. In working with furniture I have to surrender to the slow, patient demands of wood; I forget the demands of people and their sometimes unreasonable expectations of me. I love working with wood as I love writing, and from both I learn more about who I am than in tasks that seem so important because others say they are.

I touch the smooth oak finish of this dresser and look out across the rain-smoothed roofs of Pleasant Street, and praise rises spontaneously in my soul. "Be praised, my Lord, through all that you have made. Be praised through this wood which is making me whole again." And if anyone asks me what I am doing here, I may have the courage to say, "Listening to wood."

The Man in the Window

He is always there, sitting by the window of his second-floor apartment, framed by the chipped and fading gray paint that covers most of the old bricks of the houses down here. He waves and greets me whenever I leave, and sometimes he is still there in the evening when I return. He has become a part of my life, this black man, this man in the window.

Somehow, taking him to my heart is what I am all about as a Franciscan. And the distance at which I keep him is the distance between God and me. The Franciscan way is the way of embracing and taking to your heart all of God's people. Francis' whole social charism can be summed up in two outward thrusts, two horizontal movements: embracing the leper and preaching the Word of God. And both kinds of reaching out are made authentic only in the personal knowledge of Jesus Christ. To know Christ Jesus is to be a healer and a bearer of the Good News of salvation.

My friend in the window is a leper only because everyone other than myself is a leper, someone held at a distance, until I take him to my heart and embrace him in the love which is Christ Jesus. And if I am a true follower of Francis of Assisi, I do not announce the Good News to the man in the window or anyone else until I have first taken him to my heart and surrounded him with the love that makes it possible for him to hear the word of God.

Any training in ministry and theology that I have is valid only to the extent that it enables me to take this man to my heart and tell him who he really is, or perhaps more realistically, to listen to him tell me who I really am. Evangelization is a two-way street. We must hear as much, or more, than we announce, preach only where we have listened.

The Lord has already been at work in people before we enter their lives, and the Franciscan knows that intuitively. The Franciscan is a person of apocalyptic living who takes to heart Saint John's words in Revelation: "And the one who was seated on the throne said, 'See, I am making all things new.' Also he said to me, 'Write this, for these words are trustworthy and true.' Then he said to me, 'It is done!' " (21:5-6a).

The new earth is already here and if, like Francis, we take all our brothers and sisters in our arms and embrace them, both they and we will know it is true. That "it is done" is revealed in what happens when we reach out to love. The man in the window reminds me daily how far I am from that authentic Franciscan loving, for he sits in a second-floor window and I walk the streets beneath him. The Lord will lift me up to his level only if I am willing to let go and take to my heart that lonely man of the window.

Autumn Rain

Insular weather. A fall rain is graying the sky and streets outside my third-floor room. Pleasant Street is running with leavings from yesterday's market, and the few cars scattered through the parking lot give it the feel of a stadium after a game.

Weather like this is always thinking weather for me, and I remember a remark of an old black man a few days ago. I was walking down Pleasant Street on a brisk, threatening morning and mentioned to him that it sure had turned cold. "Yes, but it may get better, you know." His response triggered something in me, and I realized that everything he ever said to me was optimistic, with always a rise of hope in his voice. That little rise lifted my day immediately, and I thanked God for people like him.

When I think of Francis of Assisi now, the sound of the old man's voice rising rings in my mind. There is something ascending about Francis and his charism. He lived and moved in the real world with all its difficulty and ambiguity, but something inside was always lifting his world to the level of song. There is a book of poetry by Maya Angelou whose theme expresses succinctly the Franciscan attitude as I see it: and again I rise. No matter what happens in life, no matter how low they fall, the Resurrection has so penetrated their souls that the followers of Francis cry out, "And again we rise!"

I stretch and look out my window for a moment, and there in the bare branches of the elm tree in front of Saint John's lonely spire are nine birds clumped together. They are too far away for me to distinguish what kind of birds they are, but it doesn't matter. They have risen from these dark streets and have winged heavenward, lifting our eyes with them, reminding us we can all lift our minds and hearts to the summit of whatever gives us perspective in life.

For Saint Francis that summit is in the heart where God dwells, and he it is who makes all rising possible. Francis says to his brothers and sisters, "At all times and seasons, in every country and place, every day and all day, we must have a true and humble faith, and keep him in our hearts, where we must love, honor, adore, serve, praise and bless, glorify and acclaim, magnify and thank, the most high supreme and eternal God,

Three and One, Father, Son and Holy Spirit, Creator of all and Savior of those who believe in him, who hope in him, and who love him; without beginning and without end, he is unchangeable, invisible, indescribable and ineffable, incomprehensible, unfathomable, blessed and worthy of all praise, glorious, exalted, sublime, most high, kind, lovable, delightful and utterly desirable beyond all else, for ever and ever."

Besides being quite a sentence for a man who was supposedly unsophisticated and unlearned, these words of Saint Francis are charged with enthusiasm and joy. You can almost hear the rise in his voice. God is in our hearts! If we keep God there, then yes, Maya Angelou, it is true: And again we rise, again and again and again. And the reason for our rising is the Resurrection of him who is eternal rising, eternal ascending to the Father.

Peanut Man

Today is December 1. It is a light, bright day and the sun is hitting the leaves of my window geranium so that the leaves seem transparent. I remember to water my plants. And I remember to let the light in again, to try to make the words transparent, to let the light penetrate memory, brightening what is dull and hidden into the delicate outlines of the pattern God has woven into all experience. And he immediately comes to mind, the peanut man of my youth.

He was always there, a vivid silhouette from my high school days. We would occasionally be allowed off the seminary grounds for an excursion into downtown Cincinnati and there he would be: stovepipe hat, bow tie, pushing his two-wheeled cart through the city streets. He became through the years a permanent fixture at the Reds' games, a personality as popular as any star who played in Crosley Field and later in Riverfront Stadium.

Last week as I was walking the neighborhood, I rounded the corner of Elm and Elder, and there he was, looking for all his years as healthy as ever, sporting a stylish stovepipe, his bow tie saluting passersby, a huge box of peanuts at his foot and his ever-present school bell at his side. He sat in a wheelchair, an empty pant leg flapping in the cold November wind. I couldn't help but stare at this vision out of my youth.

"Some peanuts, young man?"

Not to buy a bag of peanuts from this man would have been like denying my own grandfather. I paid the exorbitant half dollar for a wee bag and stood there wanting to talk. I had never spoken to him in my life, so I said casually and clumsily, "How old is that hat?"

"Oh, just a couple a years. Have a new one at home, from Germany, don't find 'em here anymores."

"I haven't seen you for a while."

"No, I live up in Mt. Healthy since I lost my leg. Had a good summer at the ballpark, though, this year."

"Guess you've been to a lot of games."

"Son, I'm eighty-nine years old. Been selling peanuts forty-six years here in the city and before that I was selling forty years in the country."

I didn't know about his arithmetic, but his enthusiasm for peanuts hadn't waned. He asked me to run over to one of the stands and price the green beans.

"I need four pounds and tell them I'm a crippled old man," he said with a wry smile.

The schoolboy in me came out, and I ran over to the stand and bought four pounds of green beans for $1.35, and I remembered something Pablo Picasso said in his nineties: "It takes a long time to grow young."

Wasting Time

A friend of mine has been trying mightily to make me waste time, to put off till tomorrow what I usually do today. At first I resented her efforts, but because of our friendship and my trust in her wisdom I have been giving in and spending time walking, staring out windows and even watching TV—something I consider the ultimate waste of time.

And it has been good for me. I have been surprised by the realization that I get as much work done as ever and I am becoming comfortable with not always having to be doing something useful. Only a friend could accomplish this kind of change in me, for, left to ourselves, we are our own worst counselors. I have seen many people who are workaholics but I failed to see the same trait in myself.

There is so much satisfaction in work we enjoy doing or work that has become a habit with us that we don't see that our compulsion for work is depriving us of living. We begin to neglect the small but significant human courtesies, like visiting friends in the hospital or just dropping by a neighbor's home to say hello. Or even more importantly, we begin to neglect rituals and ceremonies important to our families, like Thanksgiving and Christmas, weddings or anniversaries. All of this happens because, as we say, we are too tired when we come home from work.

Whenever I start overworking again, I visit the little post office around the corner from our friary. I talk to the postmistress and observe her talking gently to the people of the neighborhood. She always has time for them, even during the Christmas rush. It is so rare to find someone personable behind a government counter today that I relish my moments at the post office.

The other day as I was waiting around to buy Christmas stamps, an old woman wheeled in a little red wagon with a huge, poorly wrapped package balanced precariously over its sides. Instead of scolding the woman for not wrapping the package well, the postmistress said in a neighborly, domestic tone, "My goodness, you must have come a long way with that package!" I almost hugged her when I saw the smile that her remark brought to the old woman's face. And when I got to the window and handed her a five-dollar bill and she didn't have change, she said, "Just come in and pay me sometime when you have thirty-five cents, okay?"

Today when I returned the money, there was a bowl of Christmas candy at her window and people would take a piece, only one, and thank her. Only someone relaxed about life and work could run an inner-city post office and make people happy with the U.S. Postal Service! And only someone relaxed about life and work can preach the gospel and convince people that it really is Good News!

Poverty and Patience

Always there are the long waits and the condescending looks and the humiliation of rejection. And in winter, the fear that you will freeze or that you won't have the bus fare to get to work and it will be snowing or sleeting and impossible to make it there on foot. And if Manpower calls with a job opening, your phone will be disconnected or if they get through to you and you find a way to get to work, someone will yell at you for looking unkempt and dirty. Or your accent will make you sound ignorant and you will be ignored the way you are in stores when you're trying to get someone to wait on you. And the greatest fear of all: If you get sick, how can you pay the doctor and hospital bills and how much humiliation will be involved in getting financial help from some agency?

These are the cries of poverty that I have heard since coming to Pleasant Street, and they are anything but pleasant. There are no "simple joys of poverty" down here. That kind of attitude I have never experienced in the inner city. In fact the only time I have heard of the "simple joys of poverty" has been when talking with someone once rich who has renounced wealth and freely embraced poverty as a way of life. Down here poverty is a way of life already and people long to get out of it. But fear and frustration and humiliation and bureaucracy make it easier to resign yourself to the misery of being poor.

One man I visited in the hospital looked back in terror when I asked him if I could bless him. "How much will it cost, Father? I don't have nuthin'.'" People on Pleasant Street wake up in the morning worrying about money, and they go to bed at night no richer for all their worry.

A young girl I know finally got her call from Manpower to work at a major company here. She was so excited she didn't sleep all night for fear of not waking up on time. I loaned her our '67 Volkswagen for the day and was sitting in my room praying for her when the phone rang at 8:00 a.m. She was in tears. "They yelled at me 'cause I couldn't find the right building." I knew then I should have gone with her; but after I looked at the instructions, it wouldn't have made any difference. Einstein couldn't have figured them out.

I knew it wasn't just not being able to find the building. She looked poor. She was wearing jeans and an old 1945 woman's coat too big for her which I had found in a church poverty booth. She wore the coat like a new mink because I had given it to her, but the company receptionist made her feel it was cheap. She still has the coat, but she doesn't have the job.

Poverty means learning to live with frustration and inconvenience. It means either patient endurance or violent striking back. Most of the people I know are the patient ones. There is one man from Harlan County, Kentucky, who has an accent thicker than down-home gravy and who is working here for a year or two while studying to become a lay missionary to the hill people. He has a college degree already, but he purposely cultivates his accent to see how people react to him when he tries to get a job and he dresses as poorly as he can to understand from the inside what his people suffer.

And this is not "show." He is the poorest man I know. He told me the other day that the only way to understand people is to change clothes with them the way Saint Francis did when he exchanged clothes with the beggar in Rome and spent the day begging from pilgrims. He told me to put on the worst clothes I could find and then go into the same stores and see what happens. I didn't do that because for me it would have been merely an experiment, play acting. I am not one of the poorest of the poor. He is.

His suggestion did, however, make me think about my vow of poverty and what it should mean. The only inconvenience I experience is having to ask permission and trying to live simply, but that is a lot different from not knowing how I'm going to make it through the day. Nor would I voluntarily embrace that kind of poverty; it is destitution and I would rather try to free people from destitution than embrace it.

Material poverty is very real down here, and its effects are so devastating that I don't think I could ever again romanticize poverty or agree with anyone who looks upon the poor as innocents who delight in the joys of simple living. "Simple living" is for those with money in the bank to back them up when simplicity becomes complicated, or to bail them out when the collectors come around, or to give them the security it takes to make "poverty" simple and joyful.

I have some wealthy friends in England who have built small huts on their estate for people who want to live a simple life of prayer and return to the soil. I received a letter from one of them not too long ago in which she wrote, "It's amazing how much money it takes to live simply."

Miss Susie

"One-on-one neighboring would change the world," I said to myself as I took Miss Susie to the Cincinnati Gas and Electric Company this morning at 8:00. She was afraid to take the bus because she is eighty years old and arthritic and hasn't left Pleasant Street for a long time. Her bill read $300.00, and she was afraid it wasn't a mistake.

There was a parking spot right in front of the Gas and Electric Company, and I went into a little restaurant for breakfast while I waited for Susie. She was out, mistake corrected, by 8:25 and we were home by 8:35. An errand that would have taken her a whole morning of waiting for the right bus and riding the bus and not knowing where to get off was over. A load of anxiety for her old heart was prevented by a simple ride to and from the Gas and Electric Company.

If a middle-class family lived next to a poor family all over the world and people cared for only one neighbor, we would live in a different world, a better world. There would be little need for social services and welfare then, and there would be no waiting in line to see the social worker. The great anxiety of the poor is in the waiting, the fear that they will stand all day in a line that has no end, that at the other end there will be no help for them or a further delay. And they fear that the social worker will be tired and frustrated when their turn finally comes. That is why everyone needs one poor neighbor only. As soon as there are two, there is a waiting line.

I know this sounds utopian, but if everyone who reads these words would adopt one poor family, the result would be more astounding than hundreds of government programs. In a government of the people only the people can make anything better or worse. Most of my life I have lived in suburbia sheltered from the pain of people like Susie. Oh, I cared about the poor in a general way, but I didn't know any Miss Susies. And now I understand that everyone needs a Miss Susie to love and cherish to keep life from being futile.

Miss Susie helps me far more than I help her. Every time she asks me even the smallest favor she worries that she is upsetting my plans for the day. And I think about my plans, my work, and I realize again how petty they are and how unimportant most of what we do really is. Susie's very presence reminds me how important it is to be human.

Loving is not an abstract idea; loving is for and about individual people who make each other whole by caring. Nothing I will ever do in life will be more important than taking Miss Susie to the Gas and Electric Company. She makes Pleasant Street Friary a friary. Without her there would be no sunshine here, and we would think unimportant things are important.

Postscript

"Displacement" is the big word now. Everyone on Pleasant Street is afraid of being moved out into the street to make way for renovated town houses. It is happening a few blocks away and we all know it's coming here too.

I see it beginning in the lot below my window. It used to be a sand lot; now they've paved it and put in trees and parking meters. They say it is all for Findlay Market patrons, but folks down here don't believe them.

The only ones who are happy are the kids; they have a new parking lot to skate on. Right now there are two girls skating around, one with a skate on her right foot and the other with the left skate. The workers have left some pipes stacked together and the kids have invented a game of throwing rocks through the pipes at a large board on the other side, their homemade target. They gather an appreciative audience on warm evenings when people sit on their steps to chat and smoke. The dogs, too, seem to like the posts they have driven into the ground.

The whole prospect of displacement disturbs me because I don't know what it all means and I am confused about the morality of what is happening. It is unjust to displace the poor, but are those people immoral who want to renew the inner city? Is financial gain the only motivation here? Perhaps the most important thing is to ensure the rights of the poor, to be sure they have a voice, that their rights are taken into consideration before any move is made. But what do we do in the meantime?

I like to think that the city leaders will pass some ordinance to insure the rights of the people who are my neighbors, but I've been around politics long enough to know that the initiative will have to come from the people themselves. And around here people are tired and frustrated and don't trust politics. So somebody will have to take the initiative for them. I wonder if somebody will. What will I do this time?

I look at Robert Frost's poem framed on my wall:

I shall be telling this with a sigh
Somewhere ages and ages hence:
Two roads diverged in a wood, and I—
I took the one less traveled by
And that has made all the difference.

The Almond Tree Speaks
(1994)

Alpha and Omega

I can't
You must
I'm yours
Show me the way

— Oscar Romero,
from the
movie, *Romero*

From my earliest years I have struggled to learn how to pray.
I've read books on prayer, sought the advice of spiritual
directors, embarked on exercises and programs of prayer, only
to return again and again to the sobering reality that prayer is
quite simply a gift. I cannot learn it or earn it. I can only
receive it from God. I can only make it easier for God to find
me.

This does not mean that prayer is something that comes out of
the clouds, so to speak. Rather, the gift of prayer usually comes
to us while we're "going through the motions" of praying. If we
continue to practice praying, like a musician practicing scales,
our trying to pray becomes the arena where real prayer can
happen. You get the gift by hanging around where the gift is
handed out.

It's hard to imagine an athlete finding his or her gift by
spending days hanging around symphony orchestras, listening
to musicians rehearse. In trying to find your own gift, you
frequent those places where like people have found and are still
finding theirs. Skiers spend time on slopes, writers spend time
with words, pray-ers spend time with prayers.

The gift of prayer usually begins with the saying of prayers, prayers we learn from others or read from books. Those words lead us into a world where prayer as God's gift is offered us. Like everything else worthwhile, the gift of prayer comes to most of us while we're working at praying.

But these are abstract statements. The way of knowing is concrete, so the best way of talking about prayer is to share what prayer is and has been for me and others who try to say how it is with them in prayer.

I remember, as a young boy growing up in the forties and early fifties, loving prayer books, collections of prayers like the Catholic Church's official compendium of prayers, *The Raccolta*. I would hold them reverently, their cool leather covers and Bible-thin pages precious to my touch. I was convinced that somewhere in those pages I would find God. God was hidden in the *words* of prayer. If only I could grasp them, I thought, or say them right, the formulas of those prayer books would make God present to me, or at least to my mind. God's face would emerge from the images the words were imprinting on my mind's screen as I reverently read or recited them aloud. Concentrate, I would tell myself, think! The words will bring you God.

But the words did not bring me God—they only led me into longing for what they represented. It was that way for me because I am one who loves words. But what about those for whom words do not matter as much as what they see and hear and touch and feel and smell? I can only suppose that, just as words led me into that sacred space where prayer could happen, so the objects of others' loves bring them to their sacred space, as well. One who loves the out-of-doors, for example, will find God speaking in the sights and sounds and smells of nature.

God can speak to us anywhere, of course, and does. But our normal, day-by-day speaking with God usually happens not when and where we're self-absorbed, but where we are most drawn out of ourselves toward something other that is the focus of our interest. This presumes that whatever that interest is, we allow God to speak to us through it, that we are open to God speaking through our interests and loves. One person I know feels closest to God while fishing; another, while ironing clothes or cooking.

It is important to mention at this point that my own penchant for words is not the only reason for starting out these reflections with praying by means of words. God has chosen words to reveal himself to us, and ultimately it is the Word made flesh who is *the* revelation of God. "In the beginning was the Word," Saint John writes, "and the Word was God." It is hard to overestimate the importance of these words of John's Gospel. If in the beginning is the Word, then in the beginning when God creates heaven and earth, it is the Word that creates heaven and earth. So powerful is this Word of God that all words find their meaning in that Word, and God is where the Word is revealed in all fullness. To hang around words, therefore, is to be in that space God has chosen as his first and final revelation. The Word is the Alpha and the Omega, the first and last letters of the Greek alphabet, the beginning and end of the making of all other words.

✤ 1 ✤

'Sacraments'

I.

I'm sitting on a cliff above a small trout stream in northern Arizona. Above me is the Tonto Rim and all around me are pine trees and mountain oak and, here and there, an occasional laurel tree. I look down at the stream where butterflies, white and yellow and orange, beat their silent wings up and down, back and forth across the water. Cows munch grass at the edges of the stream and chickadees break the morning quiet with their busy, "chickadee-dee-dee." The only other sound is an occasional caw of a crow in flight downstream.

Silent and graceful as the flies it mimics is my father's fishing line moving back and forth across the stream in long, languorous arcs. My father moves through the water with a limp he acquired in a foot operation botched by a surgeon not as careful with his knife as Dad is with his fly rod.

I watch him limp downstream, his sloppy canvas hat pulled low on his head, his wader boots slipping and bumping against wayward rocks; and all the while the rod moves expertly in his hand. I am reminded of Pablo Casals at ninety holding his cello with young hands after having been helped onto the stage.

Back home my mother, crippled with arthritis, with no peripheral vision after cataract surgery that would not allow for implants, holds her polenta spoon and turns the hardening corn meal over and over, forming it into a firm, cake-like ball. Polenta is the northern Italian peasant's staple; but for us, from as far back as I can remember, polenta has been *the* delicacy of our table. Garnished with mother's sauce and served with deer, quail, doves or pheasant, which my father's hunting has always supplied, polenta is one of the "sacraments" of our family.

I use the word *sacrament* here because for me polenta is more than food. It is a symbol of my mother, of all the love and skill she puts into everything she cooks. Cooking is an external sign of everything profound, and even supernatural, that motivates what she does. Like my father's fly rod, the polenta spoon (which my father fashioned from a hickory axe handle) is for me a symbol of interior values and of craft as finely honed and as seriously practiced as Ernest Hemingway's prose, Emily Dickinson's verse.

Like Hemingway's or Dickinson's writing, my father's fishing and my mother's cooking are something they *need* to do. They are compelled by something within to express themselves variously by fishing rod and polenta spoon—two dominant symbols of love and passion made concrete by a lifetime of practice, sacrifice and inner compulsion.

Serious business, this fishing and cooking. And yet, it manifests itself as play, so that neither my mother nor my father are otherwise so much relaxed and renewed as after a hard day's work at this kind of play.

II.

Sometimes, forms of self-expression complement one another. It is my father's trout that my mother cooks, his deer and pheasant and quail that garnish the polenta loaf that is the "eucharist" of Mother's table.

I am using the word *eucharist* here metaphorically for something which I invest with special value. A stone, for example, is a stone, but if I invest it with added value and meaning by making it a symbol of Christ, the Rock, the Cornerstone of my faith, then a stone becomes something more than a stone. That is why Saint Francis of Assisi reverences all of creation as somehow "sacramental." Air is sacramental because Jesus breathed it. Fire is sacramental because Jesus said he came to cast fire upon the earth and he himself was a living fire. Water is sacramental because Jesus was baptized in the Jordan and because he said there was living water flowing out of him. Earth is sacramental because Jesus walked the earth and slept upon it and was buried within it.

The polenta loaf is sacramental for me because of all the value and meaning it contains for me. What is sacramental becomes so because of what God or we have put into it. Bread and wine, for example, become sacramental because Jesus makes them the vehicles of his own body and blood. He transforms them into something more than bread and wine, not just by investing them with value, but, in this instance, by transubstantiating bread and wine literally into his own body and blood. It is only by analogy to this true Sacrament, this Eucharist, that my mother's polenta loaf becomes sacramental. It contains for me all my mother's love and sacrifice and suffering; it becomes her sacrificial offering to God, consumed by others, feeding them with her own outpoured life.

❖ 2 ❖
Of Books and Pens

It is Sunday morning in February. The gray Cincinnati sky shawls my view through the window of the Mt. Adams Gold Star Chili parlor. (I am drinking coffee and reading Colette's *My Mother's House* and *Sido*, in a slender Penguin edition that takes me back to a Paris summer....)

Gregory and I (fourteen years after we worked together on *Walk in Beauty*) are in Paris walking the rainy July streets. We've just come from Père LaChaise Cemetery where we scattered flowers extravagantly on Colette's grave, on Chopin's, and of course on the grave of Abelard and Heloise. We are staring open-mouthed at the incredible tulips in the window of La Chaume. Like sentinels, tall and slender and arrogant, they forbid entry to that elegant Parisian flower shop whose window sign warns in no uncertain terms that the passerby should not even think of entering without purchasing *something*. So we do not enter, but bid adieu to the tulips and perfect roses with their soft seduction and walk around the corner to W.H. Smith's Bookstore, where I purchase this affordable Penguin. It is inscribed, "7/22/88 W.H. Smith, Paris."

It begins to rain harder while we are in the bookstore, and we come out into a driving rain that would have crushed and turned Gene Kelly's umbrella inside out. But Gregory is determined I am to see "his" pen shop and buy an adaptor for the cartridge Waterman fountain pen I purchased earlier in Rieti, Italy. We walk on in the rain, and I keep thinking of Colette looking out her windows from her room in the Palais Royale. She would know how to write the rain so we could feel it; she would see it through her transparent words that seem at first opaque like the curtained windows which I scanned from the rose-lined paths of the Palais Royale the day before.

The pen shop is open—rows and rows of Waterman and Mont Blanc and Pelican pens waiting for some hand to lift their delicate barrels and begin the simple, yet mysterious act of shaping letters into words becoming sentences becoming tulips and roses and rain falling in clear syllables from the clouded dome that covers Paris.

I want a pen for Colette, for a souvenir of that day of flowers and tombstones and rain. But I withhold from some vague parsimony. Is it Abelard, that sometime renegade Dominican, who reminds me I am not a character out of Colette's human bestiary, but a Franciscan who should be content with a Penguin paperback and a small adaptor to transform the cartridge-holding Waterman into a pen that will drink from my bottle of ink? My pen cost about $7.00 in Rieti, a poor person's Waterman, and I'm not sure I can purchase cartridges for it in Cincinnati. I can, it turns out, and I've not used the adaptor, though I carry it about with me like a relic in the inside pocket of my blue jacket. It smells of La Chaume roses and Paris rain and reminds me of that last day in Paris and of Gregory's 102-degree temperature when we return that night to the friary on Rue Marie Rose.

Gregory falls into bed and wills away his fever for our plane trip back to New York, and I go out walking alone, out the front door, past the bronze-plaqued house where Lenin lived and around the corner to look for a patisserie where I can purchase a grand crème and croissant the following morning. I am busily reconnoitering when I look up and see a couple embracing in a window whose velvet curtains are pulled carelessly to the side.

In my inner eye they become Lea and Cheri in Colette's novel, *Cheri*, a final image of the jewelled and scarved face of Paris.

What amazes me about this little piece of writing is how much I remember and what I remember. Is it because I am reading Colette that I remember things like the rain and the flowers? My memory focuses in on things she would have seen, like the couple in the window who reminded me of Lea and Cheri, who made me see Paris jewelled and scarved.

The whole piece, though I did not intend it when I began writing, becomes an act of thanksgiving for Colette, for her talent, her pain, the grueling work that writing was for her, the whole great and sensitive soul of her. I pray for her; I thank God for her.

The kinds of associations I make in this piece, triggered by a simple inscription in a book, show, I hope, something of how the creative process works. No great inspiration seizes me, nor does the muse visit me. Rather, the very act of writing becomes the inspiration; the associations happen on the page, associations that surprise me into writing something I never intended to write, and which reveals things I didn't know before, like how important Colette's writing is to me, how much I admire and revere her. Unanticipated by me, Colette emerges as a focus of gratitude and praise of God for the gift of her life and her writing.

✧ 3 ✧

Mystical Words

I believe that what the mystic does for us is make real the conjugal language of the Bible. God speaks again and again of himself as bridegroom and Israel as bride; Jesus speaks of the wedding feast of heaven, of the bridegroom coming and of us wise or foolish virgins waiting, prepared or not.

What makes us virgins is how we wait—Are we ready, our lamps trimmed, letting nothing or no one distract us from the bridegroom's coming? The mystic is the prudent virgin who waits, her eyes fixed upon the Lord whose coming, like all his visitations, is indeed that of a bridegroom and is experienced as such by the virgin become bride.

Saint Clare of Assisi is one such virgin. From her letters to Saint Agnes of Prague, I have fashioned this poem that incorporates the conjugal language that Saint Clare herself uses in her own letters to Saint Agnes.

The Letters of Clare to Agnes of Prague

And Clare takes up her pen.
    She dips it in the black
        indelible liquid.
She draws the letters that form the words
    that name the way
        into the Bridal Chamber,
to the place of waiting
    for that soundless step
        that arrives without walking,

without opening or closing doors
  without movement
    except the movement of her heart,
  the Bride hearing no sound
    yet knowing he's there
      beyond the hearing.

He—the paradox—in whose embrace is union and virginity, in whose touch is chastity sealed. The words flow from the pen, her hand moving where her heart leads—farther into the room where he adorns her breast with precious stones, pierces her ears with gems shimmering like blossoms in springtime. His left arm circles her waist, his right circles her head with a crown, golden for holiness. It is the Crucified Christ who steals thus into her bedroom, with whom she merges as with her own image in the mirror that is the crucifix, the corpus like the mirror's bronze disk convex with desire. Can she write what she sees?

It is herself she sees in Him
  whose embrace, though rough and poor
    as the unbleached wool she wears,
  is as familiar as her own arms
    wrapped round her shivering body
      standing in the dormitory's frigid morning.

She writes:
  Gaze into that mirror each day
    until you see your own face within it.
  That contemplation in which Jesus' face
    becomes your own,
      adorns your whole body
  with the flowers and garments
    that are all the virtues:

At the border of the mirror
the swaddling clothes of poverty;
    at the surface, the laborer's tunic of humility;
        in the depth of the mirror
the nakedness of Love
    hanging from the wood of the cross,
        Love Who's become the mirror of those
who long to mount the cross with Him,
    who cry out,
        Draw me after You.
I will run and not tire,
    till You bring me into the wine-cellar,
        till Your left hand is under my head
and Your right hand embraces me happily
    and You kiss me
        with the happiest kiss of Your mouth.

❖ 4 ❖

Prayer Words

Dawn Boy says, "Beauty all around me. With Beauty I wander.
On the beautiful trail am I. With Beauty I wander." These lines
from the first song of Dawn Boy in the Navajo "Night Chant"
use the same primal language that Saint Francis of Assisi uses
in his "Canticle of Brother Sun." Like Dawn Boy, Saint Francis
sees beauty all around him and praise rises spontaneously to his
lips, though Saint Francis' praise is not of beauty, but of God
through all creation.

In an effort to combine the language of the Navajo chants with
Christian theology, the Franciscan ethnologist Berard Haile

composed a lovely Navajo prayer. It echoes the rhythms of a Navajo chant, even in the English translation which Father Berard made of his own Navajo original:

Jesus, God's son, my older brother, come to me.
From your home, from heaven, from there come to
me.
Your Father's home, from God's home, from heaven,
from there come to me.
God's spirit's home, from heaven, from there come to
me.
My Jesus, my God, come to me.
From heaven, from the sky hole, from there come to
me.
On earth where you were born, from there come to
me.
My home, along the trail leading to it, come and stand
with me.
My home, along the center of the room of it, come and
stand with me.
"My older brother, here is my home," I said to him.
"My younger brother (sister), here your home happens
to be," he said to me.
"Now here you will stay," I said to him.
"Now here with you I will certainly stay," he said to
me.
"My legs, for me you will watch over them," I said to
him.
"My body, for me you will watch over it," I said to
him.
"My arms, for me you will watch over them," I said to
him.
"My head, for me you will watch over it," I said to
him.

"My soul, for me you will watch over it," I said to him.
"My thoughts, for me you will watch over them," I said
  to him.
Before me, pleasant may it be in life.
Behind me, pleasant may it be in life.
Below me, pleasant may it be in life.
Above me, pleasant may it be in life.
In all my surroundings, pleasant may it be in life.
My sins, in my interior there shall be none.
Jesus, my older brother, come to me.
My Jesus, my God, come to me.

There is a specificity, a concreteness, in this Navajo way of
praying that is very healing, as is the chantlike repetition, so
characteristic of Native American poetry. In the Navajo
"Night Chant," for example, the singer chants:

Happily my interior becomes cool,
Happily my head becomes cool,
Happily my legs regain their power,
Happily for me the spell is taken off!
Happily may I walk in beauty....

Repetition and praying specifically, that is, naming exactly
what we are praying for (or over), are the most ancient of
prayer forms. It is the way the Psalmist prays. It is the way of
the Book of Daniel, especially in the canticle of the three
youths in the fiery furnace.

Sun and moon! bless the Lord:
give glory and eternal praise to him.
Stars of heaven! bless the Lord:
give glory and eternal praise to him.
Showers and dews! all bless the Lord:

give glory and eternal praise to him.
Winds! all bless the Lord:
give glory and eternal praise to him.
Fire and heat! bless the Lord:
give glory and eternal praise to him.
Cold and heat! bless the Lord:
give glory and eternal praise to him. (Daniel 3:62-67)

This kind of naming and the repeated, "Give glory and eternal praise to him," sum up the way of praise and thanksgiving. Praying like this leads me to pray:

For this bright, cool morning, bless the Lord.
For this notebook and pen, bless the Lord.
For these thoughts and feelings, bless the Lord.
For the way the pen moves, bless the Lord.
For the soft yellow paper, bless the Lord.
For the way the paper receives the words, bless the
   Lord.

As I continue naming, I become aware of all God's countless blessings around me and within me and what began as a boring, blah morning is transformed by the words of my praying.

The same concrete naming is involved in healing prayer, as well:

Your deeds, O Lord, have made me glad;
for the work of your hands I shout with joy.
To me you give the wild-ox's strength;
you anoint me with purest oil. (Psalm 92)

Notice that the psalmist prays here of a completed act: God has *already* given him the wild-ox's strength, anointed him with purest oil. He does not beg for it to happen. He gives thanks that it is indeed happening. And this, too, is the way of prayer. As Jesus says, "So I tell you, whatever you ask for in prayer, believe that you *have received* it, and it will be yours" (Mark 11:24).

These words indicate to me that I should not only pray with great anguish, "O God, please heal my ulcer, please, God," but also and perhaps more effectively, I should pray with joy of heart, "Thank you, Lord, that your healing touch is even now healing my ulcer." Right here, of course, is where all the red flags go up. Am I being presumptuous? Am I just praying my own wishful thinking, my own will? Am I praying an illusion? What if I'm *not* healed? Does that mean I didn't pray right? Was my thanking God for healing me now just a veiled way of forcing God's hand, a sort of Divine superstition that says, "If I do this, the result will follow automatically"? Magic, after all, is something we do want to believe in.

There is a poem by Philip Larkin that expresses what I am trying to say in these caveats better than I can, a poem that articulates our modern skepticism about faith healing, while at the same time conveying a profound compassion and longing that the "illusion" of faith-healing might be true.

Faith Healing

Slowly the women file to where he stands
Upright in rimless glasses, silver hair,
Dark suit, white collar. Stewards tirelessly
Persuade them onwards to his voice and hands,
Within whose warm spring rain of loving care
Each dwells some twenty seconds. *Now, dear child,*

What's wrong, the deep American voice demands,
And, scarcely pausing, goes into a prayer
Directing God about this eye, that knee.
Their heads are clasped abruptly; then, exiled

Like losing thoughts, they go in silence; some
Sheepishly stray, not back into their lives
Just yet; but some stay stiff, twitching and loud
With deep hoarse tears, as if a kind of dumb
And idiot child within them still survives
To re-awake at kindness, thinking a voice
At last calls them alone, that hands have come
To lift and lighten; and such joy arrives
Their thick tongues blort, their eyes squeeze grief, a
    crowd
Of huge unheard answers jam and rejoice—

What's wrong! Moustached in flowered frocks they
    shake:
By now, all's wrong. In everyone there sleeps
A sense of life lived according to love.
To some it means the difference they could make
By loving others, but across most it sweeps
As all they might have done had they been loved.
That nothing cures. An immense slackening ache,
As when, thawing, the rigid landscape weeps,
Spreads slowly through them—that, and the voice
    above
Saying, *Dear child*, and all time has disproved.[1]

Larkin's language here is quite as specific as that of Dawn Boy
and the Hebrew poets. But it is infected with a doubt that
makes the final line so sad: "Saying, 'Dear child,' and all time
has disproved."

Don't we feel like that from time to time, feel that our own experience disproves those encouraging words that God does heal, that God wants to heal, that if we believe that God has already healed us, then we *are* healed? How do we reconcile Jesus' words with what all time disproves? How do we pray about this?

As I pondered these questions, the Book of Job leaped into my mind as *the* model for a way of praying that encompasses both of these realities. In Job we have naming and thanksgiving and doubt and anger and questioning and healing and ultimately, we have God's answer. The Lord says to Eliphaz and his two friends: "My wrath is kindled against you...for you have not spoken of me what is right, as my servant Job has" (Job 42:7).

It is this honest Job who sings "The Canticle of the Creatures," the "Song of Dawn Boy." It is this painful journey through a dark wood of naming our doubts, of arguing and wrestling with God, that breaks into the clearing where we can sing with the Jesuit poet, Gerard Manley Hopkins:

> The world is charged with the grandeur of God.
>   It will flame out, like shining from shook foil;
>   It gathers to a greatness, like the ooze of oil
> Crushed. Why do men then now not reck his rod?
> Generations have trod, have trod, have trod;
>   And all is seared with trade; bleared, smeared
>   with toil;
>   And wears man's smudge and shares man's smell:
>   the soil
> Is bare now, nor can foot feel, being shod.
> And for all this, nature is never spent;
>   There lives the dearest freshness deep down things;
>   And though the last lights off the black West went

Oh, morning, at the brown brink eastward, springs—

Because the Holy Ghost over the bent
    World broods with warm breast and with ah!
        bright wings. ("God's Grandeur")[2]

It is when we become general, when we pray in generalities
like, "How good God is," or "Thank you, God, for everything,"
that things get fuzzy and a subtle divorce between our actual
daily living and our prayer life ensues.

All of the above still does not answer the question: Am I being
presumptuous when I say, "Thank you, God, that you are
already healing my ulcer," and then believing that because I
believe it, I am indeed healed? What are we to make of Jesus'
words assuring us that is the way to pray? It seems to me that I
am to take Jesus at his word and what happens then is the
beginning of my deepest dialogue with God. My whole
prayer-relationship with God and God's with me begins and
ends in dialogue over taking God at his word.

The psalter, like the Book of Job, is a model for this kind of
dialogue. The psalmist praises God, asks God, argues with God,
and thanks God that God is indeed faithful to his word. The
honesty of this ongoing conversation with God is the measure
of the sincerity of our prayer, and it all begins with what
happens (or does not happen) when we take God at his word.
It is the person who has engaged in this kind of dialogue with
God who finally can pray with Saint Francis:

Most High, all powerful, good Lord,
Yours is the praise, the glory and the honor,
And every blessing.
They belong to You alone,

In using the word *dialogue* in this context, I am, of course, saying that prayer is not a monologue I engage in, but that God speaks too. What does that mean? Do I hear God's voice speaking inside me? Does God have a disembodied voice that calls to me from a cloud or a tree? For me, at least, that is not the way God speaks. The way God speaks to me is what happens when I believe that whatever I ask for in prayer, I *have* received. If I perceive that I have indeed received it, then God has spoken and I give God thanks and praise. If it doesn't happen, then God has also spoken. And then we have to talk about it, or at least I have to tell God about it. What happens then is God's response which I keep talking to him about.

God speaks to me in the events of my life, and I keep telling God what I think about them, how I feel about them. It is my deepest conviction that this ongoing arguing and asking and thanking leads to the final realization that I have spoken aright, as Job did, and that God *has* been faithful to his promises to me.

It is at that moment of realization that we sing our canticle of praise, which comes, of necessity, only at the end of our journey of prayer, before we cease praying and believing, and see God face to face and *know* what before we believed. Then what all time *seemed* to disprove, is proven true—I am God's "Dear child," Dawn Child, who sings:

> Beauty all around me. With Beauty I wander.
> On the beautiful trail am I. With Beauty I wander.

✦ 5 ✦

Divine Reading

Late have I loved you, O Beauty ever ancient, ever
new, late have I loved you! You were within me, but I
was outside, and it was there that I searched for you. In
my unloveliness I plunged into the lovely things
which you created. You were with me, but I was not
with you. Created things kept me from you; yet if they
had not been in you they would not have been at all.
You called, you shouted, and you broke through my
deafness. You flashed, you shone, and you dispelled my
blindness. You breathed your fragrance on me; I drew
in breath and now I pant for you. I have tasted you,
now I hunger and thirst for more. You touched me,
and I burned for your peace.

This passage from *The Confessions of St. Augustine* is one of my
favorite passages of religious prose. It expresses the deepest
yearnings of the heart for God, and it does so in a holistic way:
embracing body and soul as a unity. Augustine's words,
summarizing the process of conversion, begin with that sense
of loss and waste that hits us so powerfully once we come to
know the living God: How late I'm coming to this—if only I
had known sooner—how many years I've wasted. And what is
it I've waited too long for? "Late have I loved *you!*" And how
blind I've been not to see that you were within me all the time
I was looking for you "out there."

"In my unloveliness I plunged into the lovely things which you
created." How ambiguous and tension-filled this sentence is,
and how true to the process of conversion, whereby we
experience ourselves (prior to knowing God) as unlovely and

as tainting the lovely things of God's creation. This is the kind of sentence, which, taken out of context, would seem to indicate that Saint Augustine is still very much a Manichaean— filled with images of himself as unclean, unlovely. But Augustine is never that simplistic. He always qualifies, sees the ambiguities, the other side of things, as the next two sentences illustrate: "You were with me, but I was not with you. Created things kept me from you; yet if they had not been in you, they would not have been at all." In other words, created things kept me from you, not because they are evil, but because I failed to see that they were in you who created and sustained them, as I failed to see that I was in you and you in me.

Then Augustine shows how God breaks through to us— through the senses: hearing, sight, smell, taste and touch. The very instruments of our former sinning become the vehicles of God's love. God becomes *the* object we long to see, hear, smell, taste and touch. God is not some remote, abstract idea, but a person capable of satisfying all our senses. God becomes more real than the things we thought were the only reality. What is inside moves outside and what is outside moves inside. What is unperceived is perceived through that which we can see, hear, touch, taste and smell.

As Augustine himself says in the paragraph previous to the one quoted above, "I sought a way to gain the strength which I needed to enjoy you. But I did not find it until I embraced the mediator between God and us, the man Christ Jesus, who is above all, God blessed forever.... He was offering the food which I lacked the strength to take, the food he had mingled with our flesh. For the Word became flesh, that your wisdom, by which you created all things might provide milk for us children." It is through the enfleshment of the Word in Christ that God is made tangible food for us, and it is through our own flesh that we see, hear, taste, touch and smell the Word, who is God blessed forever.

What I have been doing in these ruminations is interpreting a text that I love. In doing so I am explicating Augustine, but I am also revealing something about myself. For the way we read a text says as much about us as it does about the text itself. Therefore, interpreting, commenting upon a passage we love, is another way of seeing what we believe, what we are thinking.

Through these written words my own inner thoughts and feelings, my beliefs and values are revealed. I'm sure if you were to take the same passage from Augustine and write what you think the text is saying, a slightly different version would emerge—maybe a *very* different version. For we each bring something different to a text, something that is uniquely our own. As in human relationships, our own autonomy is revealed in seeking union with the other. And reading a text we love *is* an act of union. We enter into the words, we become one with them; but we retain our autonomy, as well; and this becomes evident as soon as we begin to comment on what a text means.

This careful, prayerful reading of a text was called the "Lectio Divina" in the Middle Ages, a "Divine Reading," and was considered a form of meditation, a form of prayer. Lectio Divina transforms a text (to use Martin Buber's terms) from an I-It relationship to an I-Thou relationship. The text begins to live and breathe and communicate like another person in dialogue with the reader.

In addition to leading to meditation and prayer, Lectio Divina was also a source of creativity, as the numerous medieval commentaries attest. In commenting upon Aristotle, for example, Saint Thomas Aquinas created a whole system of Christian philosophy that was uniquely his own, though it was the non-Christian Aristotle with whom he was dialoguing.

Your own creativity will emerge in much the same way if you allow yourself to comment on a text that is special, or "sacred," to you. Perhaps the words of Augustine quoted here speak to you something other than what I saw in them. You may, for example, wonder why God comes to Augustine as Beauty: Why does the passage end with the word *peace*? Is that the word you expected there? You may be struck with the fact that the whole passage is addressed to God and want to address your commentary to Augustine.

Or maybe there is another text you especially love, a text you've taped to your wall, or stuck between the pages of your Bible or prayer book. Why is it special to you, what does it say to you?

One fruitful way to begin writing about a text is to first write out the text by hand, and then continue writing *about* what you have just written. The physical act of putting words on the page makes you see connections and meanings and words you didn't notice when you merely read the text.

✣ 6 ✣

The Poetry of Praise

Each mortal thing does one thing and the same:
Deals out that being indoor each one dwells;
Selves—goes itself; myself it speaks and spells,

Crying *What I do is me: for that I came*.
                                    — Gerard Manley Hopkins

These lines are from a poem by Gerard Manley Hopkins, a Jesuit priest and poet, the centenary of whose death we are celebrating as I write these lines. Hopkins died on June 8, 1889, but it wasn't until 1918, nearly thirty years after his death, that the reading public began to be aware of the relatively small but extraordinarily original body of poetry that he left behind. If ever there was a celebrator of creation, it was Hopkins. Like a modern Saint Francis of Assisi, he sang canticles of praise to the Creator through and for all of creation. Because he is a poet, and a difficult one at that, many people steer away from Hopkins. They lose thereby the rich and beautiful sound of lines like these from "Pied Beauty":

> Glory be to God for dappled things—
>> For skies of couple-colour as a brinded cow;
>>> For rose-moles all in stipple upon trout that
>>> swim....

Or from "God's Grandeur":

> The world is charged with the grandeur of God.
> It will flame out, like shining from shook foil;
> ....
> Because the Holy Ghost over the bent
> World broods with warm breast and with ah! bright
>> wings.

A poet's power is in the sound, the intonation of the words, as much as in the meaning of the words and the images those words conjure up. This sound is something deep in the souls of those who've grown up in the Judeo-Christian tradition. The words of the Bible, for example, have a powerful rhythmic sound, a sound most of us have heard proclaimed over and over again from altars and pulpits all our lives. And that sound gets inside us, so that at least unconsciously, we feel the rhythm of the majestic biblical cadences. For this reason alone, if for no other, we are all influenced by the rhythms and sounds of words, whether we like poetry or not.

Then there are the prayers we learned as children. I can't remember any of them that don't have a strong, steady rhythm to them. That is one of the reasons we remember them. I think here of the "Our Father" and "Hail Mary," the "Litany of the Blessed Virgin Mary," with its strong, two-beat lines like, "Tower of Ivory," "Mystical Rose."

The point that all this is leading to is that the rhythm and sound of words that poetry emphasizes is a helpful means toward prayers of praise.

The psalms, especially, in the way they sound and move act like mantras on the soul. They regularize the erratic beating of our hearts, they elevate our panicked cries to song. To enter into the rhythm of the psalms is to enter into a rhythm which calms and synchronizes our hearts with the movement of the natural world around us. Praying the rhythm of the psalms is like breathing in sync with waves beating the shore. It takes us out of ourselves into an ordered, regular rhythm that acts like a metronome on the often chaotic, uneven movement of our daily lives. Poetry orders and makes music of our crazy starts and stops and goings in all directions. Poetry slows us down enough to say:

> The Lord is my shepherd; I shall not want.
> He maketh me to lie down in green pastures:

he leadeth me beside the still waters.
He restoreth my soul: he leadeth me
  in the paths of righteousness for his name's sake.
Yea, though I walk through the valley of the
  shadow of death, I will fear no evil:
    for thou art with me; thy rod and thy staff they
      comfort me.
Thou preparest a table before me in the presence
  of mine enemies: thou anointest my head
  with oil; my cup runneth over.
Surely goodness and mercy shall follow me all
  the days of my life: and I will dwell in the house
  of the LORD forever. (Psalm 23, *King James Version*)

You can't hurry those words without doing violence to them. Nor can you grasp their significance as quickly as you can read and understand the morning paper. The rhythm forces you to a slower reading, the sound consoles, the meaning seeps into your soul slowly.

It is in this slowing down that we enter into the quiet, peaceful part of ourselves from which praise arises. But first we have to do it. We have to "be still and know that I am God." The strong four beats of that line command what the meaning of the words command. The two dimensions of sound and meaning become one. And if we recite the lines over and over, they begin to do what they say, and we become still. We know that God *is* God. Then quite naturally we praise God for reminding us.

I believe that this quiet place within is the origin of this wondrous poem of praise at the beginning of this chapter. Perhaps now you will be better disposed to hear and can even bring yourself to say aloud the great words of Gerard Manley

Hopkins' "Pied Beauty":

> Glory be to God for dappled things—
>   For skies of couple-colour as a brinded cow;
>   For rose-moles all in stipple upon trout that swim;
> Fresh-firecoal chestnut-falls; finches' wings;
>   Landscape plotted and pieced—fold, fallow, and
>   plough;
>   And all trades, their gear and tackle and trim.
>
> All things counter, original, spare, strange;
>   Whatever is fickle, freckled (who knows how?)
>   With swift, slow; sweet, sour; adazzle, dim;
> He fathers-forth whose beauty is past change:
>   Praise him.

If you were able to slow down your reading and recite Hopkins' poem aloud, I'm sure you were surprised how much more of it you understood than had you read it over quickly and silently to yourself. Poetry is for saying aloud. Poetry is music written for the speaking voice.

And even if the poem made no sense to you, and you did not understand it on first reading, didn't the sound of it do something for you the way certain prayers and psalms did when you were a child and didn't quite understand what they meant, though you liked to hear them?

The music of poetry is already in us. It is innate. But to bring that music to consciousness takes some work. One of the ways to get in touch with the music of words is to memorize (Yes, that old-fashioned practice is still valid!) some poem or prayer that has moved you. It could be a psalm like Psalm 23 above, or a poem you learned as a child and have forgotten until this moment. How much of it do you still remember? Write out (and say the words aloud as you write) whatever lines are still in you—from school, from church, from something your mother or father taught you, like the Prayer to Your Guardian Angel or the Act of Contrition. You will be surprised, I think, how much rhythm is in the lines, and how strongly the rhythm of those lines affects your praying or saying the words from your heart.

❖ 7 ❖

The Spirituality of Place

The sentinels of my childhood are the red sandstone rocks that stand at attention east of Gallup, New Mexico. They've become, because of their striking prominence, capitalized—The Red Rocks. They are, after all, nothing but sandstone rocks; but because of their color and size, and the way they jut out like hulls of giant ships, they've taken on a significance beyond the simple sand they're made of, so that people speak of them as The Red Rocks of Gallup.

In my own imagination they are the remains of giant ships resting on the sandy bottom of a vast ocean that has since dried up. I've often thought that these "ships" are the reason for my love of the sea, though I was born on the desert. I remember waking once on the Greek Island of Mykonos, and, not seeing the Aegean in the distance, I thought that I was in New Mexico. The houses piled around me like a Native American Pueblo, and parched hillsides and blowing sand evoked the world of my childhood. If the Aegean would dry up, I thought, I'd be in Zuni, New Mexico.

The same kind of transformation occurs in the world of the spirit. The simple objects of our everyday lives are transfigured, not by color and size, but by their association with some sacred event. Mount Tabor, for example, is no Mount Everest in size and grandeur. But for the Christian this modest rise in the landscape towers high and radiates the glory of the transfigured Christ. Once when he walked among us, Jesus took Peter, James and John up this mountain to pray with him:

> And while he was praying, the appearance of his face changed, and his clothes became dazzling white. Suddenly they saw two men, Moses and Elijah, talking to him. They appeared in glory ....[Then] a cloud came and overshadowed them; and they were terrified as they entered the cloud. Then from the cloud came a voice that said, "This is my Son, my Chosen; listen to him!" (Luke 9:29-36)

Mount Tabor, from that moment on, becomes something more than a mountain. The kind of dynamic that occurs in this transfiguring of Mount Tabor is what changes ordinary places into sacred places. Some transfiguration has occurred, something that shapes, or figures, what is there to what is "trans," beyond. It seems valid, therefore, to speak of the spirituality of places, or the spirit of a place that draws us there.

I have known such places, and they continue to draw me and strengthen my faith as they did when I first discovered them. They are the spot where Thomas à Becket was martyred in Canterbury Cathedral, England; the grotto where Our Lady appeared to Saint Bernadette in Lourdes, France; the rose window to the right of Mary's statue in Notre Dame Cathedral in Paris; the tomb of Pope Paul VI in the crypt of St. Peter's Basilica, Rome; the tomb of Saint Thérèse in Lisieux, France;

the tomb of Saint Clare in Assisi, Italy; the tomb of the
Franciscan, Blessed John Duns Scotus in Cologne, Germany;
the statue of Mary in the lower church of the Basilica of Saint
Francis of Assisi; the black Madonna at Montserrat in Spain;
the original picture of Our Lady of Perpetual Help in Rome;
the Portiuncula, the small church Saint Francis restored with
his own hands and where he died; the grave of John Keats in
the Protestant Cemetery in Rome; the tomb of Abelard and
Heloise in Père LaChaise Cemetery, Paris; the ancient Greek
theater at Epidaurus in Greece; the agora, or market place, of
the Parthenon in Athens; the Greek Island of Delos; Canyon
de Chelley on the Navajo Reservation near Chinle, Arizona;
the Jungfrau, second highest mountain in Europe, near
Interlaaken, Switzerland; the room where John Keats died at
the foot of the Spanish steps in Rome; the room where Ernest
Hemingway wrote in Key West, Florida.

Why these places draw me and move me has much to do with
me, of course, but they also are all places that have been
transformed by something beyond the tangible—what we can
see, touch, hear, smell. These are places I've actually
experienced. Other places draw me, though I've never been
there: the Garden of Olives outside Jerusalem; Bethlehem and
Nazareth; Macchu Picchu in Peru; Mount Olympus in Greece.

All of these places connect to something inside me, to my own
soul. What these places connect to is personal to each of us,
but that these places do connect to us derives from the fact
that something of the spirit, human or divine, has transformed
the place into more than a locale or an object. Each of the
places I've mentioned has affected my spirit. Either my faith
has been strengthened, my creativity enhanced, my sense of
bonding with those who've gone before confirmed, or even, in
the case of Saint Thomas à Becket, Saint Thérèse, Saint Clare,

and John Keats, a feeling that I know them, that they are somehow communicating with me.

A few years ago, for example, I was walking with another friar along a path below the medieval Gothic church and tomb of Mary Magdalene in Vezelay, France. It was about 9:30 p.m. and still light as is customary for that part of France. Suddenly, an incredibly beautiful and melancholy bird-song startled me. It drew me almost physically into the woods where it retreated deeper and deeper.

"What *is* that bird?" I asked. "You mean you've never heard a nightingale?" I hadn't, but at the sound of the word, the bird was transfigured into John Keats. Keats was somehow in the woods drawing me with the hypnotic power of his "Ode to a Nightingale":

> Away! Away! for I will fly to thee!
>   Not charioted by Bacchus and his pards,
> But on the viewless wings of Poesy,
>   Though the dull brain perplexes and retards;
> Already with thee! tender is the night—
>   ....
> The voice I hear this passing night was heard
>   In ancient days by emperor and clown:
> Perhaps the self-same song that found a path
>   Through the sad heart of Ruth, when, sick for
> home,
>   She stood in tears amid the alien corn:
>   The same that oft-times hath
>   Charmed magic casements opening on the foam
>   Of perilous seas, in faery lands forlorn.

Forlorn! the very word is like a bell,

To toll me back from thee to my sole self!
Adieu! the Fancy cannot cheat so well
   As she is famed to do, deceiving elf.
Adieu, adieu! thy plaintive anthem fades
   Past the near meadows, over the still stream,
      Up the hill-side; and now 'tis buried deep
         In the next valley-glades:
   Was it a vision or a waking dream?
      Fled is that music—do I wake or sleep?[3]

Meanwhile, "my" nightingale had moved to the next valley-glades, as well, and the song could no longer be heard. I wondered, too, whether the nightingale's song had been a vision or a waking dream. As the music fled deeper and deeper, and more softly into the woods, I'd felt my own aloneness, as Keats did, though I walked with another friar.

Keats' poem became the nightingale and the nightingale his poem, and I felt I was in the spell of a wonderful charm. Bird-song and poem became one incantation penetrating to the depths of my soul; and as the music ceased, I thought of my own unique self, alone in the world, yes. But I was also conjoined with the nightingale, with the soul of Keats, and with the Bible's Ruth, too, who reminded me of myself standing in an Ohio cornfield so far from the maize fields of my youth, me walking a lonely path in France, so far from home.

✤ 8 ✤

Stones That Speak

I'm holding in my hands a small stone I picked from the Verde River near Payson, Arizona, where I wrote some of the pages of this book. I wonder if even a stone speaks. How long will I have to hold it and look at it to hear what it says?

In a very short time the stone says,
>Wherever you move me
>I'm still a stone.

A month later the stone added these words,
>Surrender like me.
>You'll not be alone.

Now I have a little four-line, rhymed poem that the stone spoke to me:

>Wherever you move me
>I'm still a stone.
>Surrender like me.
>You'll not be alone.

Is that all the stone will say? I don't know yet, because I've not stopped listening. But I do know something from this quatrain. Had I discarded the first two lines because they seemed foolish or too simple or naive, the last two lines wouldn't have come to me a month later. I knew if I let those lines sit and came back to them later, something further might happen on the page. And so it did. Not something great, or monumental, but something that wasn't there before, something created out of listening to a stone.

Almost three years after writing the above, I'm sitting at a window table at Inn the Wood, a restaurant on Calhoun Street, across from the University of Cincinnati. I've been ill and am drinking tea, eating poached eggs on English muffins, reading Zbigniew Herbert's *Selected Poems*. I turn the page to his poem, "Pebble."

> The pebble
> is a perfect creature
>
> equal to itself
> mindful of its limits
>
> filled exactly
> with a pebbly meaning
>
> with a scent which does not
> remind one of anything
> does not frighten anything
> away, does not arouse desire
>
> its ardour and coldness
> are just and full of dignity
>
> I feel a heavy remorse
> when I hold it in my hand
> and its noble body
> is permeated by false warmth
>
>> —Pebbles cannot be tamed
>> to the end they will look at us
>> with a calm and very clear eye.[4]

The pebble elicits a poem from Herbert, as the stone begins to elicit a poem from me. The fact that when I wrote of the stone it came out looking like a poem rather than a story or nonfiction prose, is something I don't fully understand, but I have noticed that experiences and objects find words that shape themselves into their own forms; they discover their own genre if we let them speak.

The places I wrote about in the previous chapter sometimes elicited stories from me, sometimes poems. Here, for example, are poems that grew out of places I tried to listen to.

Rome

From the hill
of the Gianicolo
Rome is quiet.
You cannot see
or hear the cars
mining her.

In Lisieux

The basilica's rounded dome
and minarets, breasts
pointed heavenward,
lie back upon the earth.
Nearby, in Carmel
on her back in wax and glass,
Thérèse, God's bride, lies ready.

The Magdalene of Vezelay

New churches
are warm.
Here, cold stones
press light
through dark glass
and summer solstice
lifts the soul
in her bright
zero arms.

Assisi, Summer Evening

I.
Like the swarm of bugs they eat
the swallows scream in heat
shaking the folds of dream
like rugs.

II.
The wheat bends in the fields
below the city walls.
The poppies are gone
and green grapes hang
heavy on the vine.
July hazes the far hills.

Why did each of these experiences elicit a poem? Was there
something inherent in the experience that was "poetic"? I
don't think so. I certainly didn't set out to write poems about
these places. I let the place speak through me and what I heard
took the shape of a poem on the page. I don't fully understand

how that happens, but I do think it has something to do with letting words find their own form, their own shape on the page.

✦ 9 ✦

Inside Your Rosary Beads

To the right of the train, antelope prance about the water holes like kiwis on the shore. Delicate. Their spindly legs ballerina-like against the green backdrop of grass. We are somewhere between Las Vegas and Raton, New Mexico, and my eyes are shifting back and forth between the sporadic small herds of antelope and the old woman across the aisle who is frantically searching her seat for something. She stands up, her disheveled white hair ragged with anxiety. Outside, another herd of antelope stand peacefully by a small water hole.

The woman searches and searches and plunges her pale hand into the crevices of the seat. Finally, she sighs and turns around, tears of joy in her eyes. I am a stranger to her, but she looks at me gratefully and says, "I have found my rosary. It was blessed by the Pope when he came to Phoenix. What would I have done if I'd lost it? I was so worried." She smiles and kisses the white beads. She leans back secure and at peace. Other antelope are standing still beside the clear water. The lady's eyes are already closed. She's sleeping, her rosary clutched in her hands.

I take out my own rosary and begin to pray, but I cannot pray for thinking: Why do I pray the rosary? Why do I continue to return to this form of prayer when other devotions from my childhood have somehow fallen by the wayside of my journey to God?

Perhaps it is because nowhere in prayer do I use my imagination more frequently than in the rosary. For me the power of the rosary's attraction is twofold: It focuses my imagination on the mysteries of our salvation, and it provides a framework for healing prayer for myself and others. When I pray the mysteries of the rosary, not only do I image the mystery of a specific event in the life of Jesus and Mary, but I place whomever I am praying for in the scene I am meditating on. For example, if I am praying the Joyful Mystery of the Visitation, I not only imagine Mary hastening into the hill country to visit her cousin Elizabeth, but I imagine someone else in Elizabeth's home, someone who needs my prayers. Then I see Mary greeting Elizabeth and Elizabeth introducing Mary to the other person in her home who needs the healing touch of the child in Mary's womb. I then imagine the person placing his or her hand on Mary's womb, and healing light and warmth begins to flow through all their being. And all the while, I am reciting the Hail Mary to myself as background music, as a mantra, that calms the soul and synchronizes my previous frenetic rhythm with the rhythm of chant-like music.

Thus, the rosary becomes a prayer of both meditation and intercession: Each of the fifteen mysteries is not only a meditation on a mystery of Christ's life, but a creative imagining of Jesus' healing power through Mary. It is a way of praying that works for me and makes the rosary the most practical way of praying Jesus' command that we love God with our whole soul and heart and mind, and our neighbor as ourselves. For in praying the rosary I focus on God, on others and on myself. We are all in each scene, each mystery of the rosary. In and through Mary we adore God, we talk with Jesus, we let him touch us and talk with us, we forgive each other, minister to one another, rejoice with Mary and Jesus, grieve with them in Jesus' Passion and death, and rise to new life with the Risen Jesus.

This is only one way of praying the rosary. It may not be the way of the woman across the aisle from me. But perhaps what I have written here on this train may offer new ideas for making the rosary more fruitful. Perhaps you can create variations on this way of praying, like imagining Mary visiting Elizabeth, whose face becomes that of a sick friend of yours; or you may "become" Mary herself hearing the angel's greeting. How do you feel hearing the angel's words, what will you do about them? Can you pick one of the mysteries of the rosary and write a scene in which you include yourself and someone you want to pray for? You may want to carry that piece of paper with you and read it over before you begin to pray the rosary.

❖ 10 ❖

Inferno

I lie here recovering from surgery. The black and white TV screen statics, the picture rolls and fades in and out with images of the Branch Davidian inferno in Waco, Texas. I blink away visions of some apocalyptic nightmare and realize I'm awake, not sleeping. What is this? Is it not only one more manifestation of irrepressible ego and of pride's unconscionable delusions—one man's private hell imposed through mind on the minds of others?

The words of Saint Francis fill the screen of my own mind: "Those who are put in charge of others should be no prouder of their office than if they had been appointed to wash the feet of their confreres. They should be no more upset at the loss of their authority than they would be if they were deprived of the task of washing feet" (Admonition IV).

How great is the distance between the washing of feet and the setting of fires whether of buildings or of violence in the hearts of others. Again Saint Francis writes, "We can never tell how patient or humble we are when everything is going well with us. But when those who should cooperate with us do the exact opposite, then we can tell. We have as much patience and humility as we have then, and no more" (Admonition XIII). And again, "Woe to that religious who, after being put in a position of authority by others, is not eager to leave it of his own free will" (Admonition XX). And on and on, quotations from Saint Francis scrambling onto the screen. And yet these, too, are words. Words influence, words brainwash, words are power in a world already too preoccupied with power. What then is the antidote to power and all its illusions? Can words save us from illusion when it is often words themselves that created the illusion?

Here I falter, realizing my own writing pad is now filled with the very words I'm questioning. My own ambivalence forces me to reach beyond words to their makers, their users; for, are not words human makings and no better or worse than the heart and mind behind them? We trust the words of Saint Francis of Assisi, we mistrust the words of David Koresh, not because of their rhetoric—both men are unlettered—but because of their makers' actions, because Saint Francis washes the feet of his followers and bathes lepers' wounds, and David Koresh arms his followers and sets fire to his own kingdom.

Again I falter rereading my own self-righteous prattle. I look up at the crucifix on the wall and see the "powerlessness" of God, who said as he hung upon the cross, "Father, forgive them, for they know not what they do," and, "Into thy hands I commend my spirit." And that is power enough for me. I ask someone to turn off the TV, now a cacophony of voices blaming others, no one forgiving, no one surrendering to anything higher than their own words.

✣ 11 ✣

My Mother's House and Polly

Shall I, like Colette, write on blue paper
Now that you are gone? And can I write
My Mother's House and *Polly*? Details
Escape me, or did they also flee Colette
Until she put blue ink to blue sheet,
The words becoming what she'd thought
She'd lost? Here goes then, the words.

In March they would come, those sandstorms that blew whistles of sand under the doors, through window cracks and down the chimney of the kitchen coal stove. Mother would put the doilies and figurines, the Navajo rugs and curtains into cedar chests. She'd cover the couch and easy chair with old sheets, and for weeks we would live with sand like bothersome dandruff everywhere. It was during March winds that I'd see my mother's exasperation, which at other times of the year she kept at bay by cleaning and cooking and working long hours at the Elite Laundry across from the Harvey House on Gallup's Main Street.

I see now how heroic those "other times" were. I'm rereading her last letters to me, and I'm bowled over by the correctness of her spelling, her grammar, her Palmer Method penmanship. From the time I left for the seminary at age fourteen till this my fifty-third year, mother wrote to me every week without fail. Reams and reams of beautiful pages from one who left school after the eighth grade to support her three younger brothers and her sister. How talented, how creative she was, and how frustrating all those years of mining towns and hard physical labor must have been.

One of mother's last letters to me recounts her experience of reading the novel *The Cardinal*, by Henry Morton Robinson. Her words are so reminiscent of Gustave Flaubert's beautiful character, Felicite, in *The Simple Heart*, that I weep to read them. They remind me of my first reading of *The Simple Heart* as a freshman in college and how I wept then too, seeing in Flaubert's Felicite the innocence and goodness and wonder that were so much a part of my mother. For example, when Felicite's beloved nephew goes to sea, Flaubert writes of her:

> Felicite's thoughts from that moment ran entirely on her nephew. On sunny days she was harassed by the idea of thirst; when there was a storm she was afraid of the lightning on his account. As she listened to the wind growling in the chimney or carrying off the slates she pictured him lashed by that same tempest, at the top of the shattered mast, with his body thrown backwards under a sheet of foam; or else...he was being eaten by savages, captured in a wood by monkeys, or dying on a desert shore. And never did she mention her anxieties.

Had I been a foreign missionary—even, I suspect when I went

away to the seminary, my mother had thoughts like those; her imagination and empathy were that keen.

In another place Flaubert has Felicite asking M. Bourais how far it was from France to Cuba, where her nephew was:

> He reached for his atlas and began explaining the longitudes; Felicite's consternation provoked a fine pedantic smile. Finally he marked with his pencil a black, imperceptible point in the indentations of an oval spot, and said as he did so, "Here it is." She bent over the map; the maze of colored lines wearied her eyes without conveying anything; and on an invitation from Bourais to tell him her difficulty she begged him to show her the house where Victor was living. Bourais threw up his arms, sneezed, and laughed immensely: a simplicity like hers was a positive joy.

My mother's simplicity was not that extreme, but her sense of wonder was. I'll never forget taking her to Westminster Abbey and Canterbury Cathedral, to Notre Dame and St. Peter's. Her awe and wonder, her imaginative re-creation of what was happening in the windows and ceilings (especially of the Sistine Chapel) was a positive joy for me. Again I am reminded of Flaubert's Felicite:

> After making a genuflexion at the door she walked up between the double row of chairs under the lofty nave, opened Mme. Aubain's pew, sat down, and began to look about her.... On a painted window in the apse the Holy Ghost looked down upon the Virgin. Another window showed her on her knees before the child Jesus, and a group carved in wood behind the

altar-shrine represented St. Michael overthrowing the dragon.

The priest began with a sketch of sacred history. The Garden, the Flood, the Tower of Babel, cities in flames, dying nations, and overturned idols passed like a dream before her eyes; and the dizzying vision left her with reverence for the Most High and fear of his wrath. Then she wept at the story of the Passion. Why they had crucified Him, when He loved the children, fed the multitudes, healed the blind, and had willed, in His meekness, to be born among the poor, on the dungheap of a stable? The sowings, harvests, wine-presses, all the familiar things the Gospel speaks of, were a part of her life. They had been made holy by God's passing; and she loved the lambs more tenderly for her love of the Lamb, and the doves because of the Holy Ghost.

She found it hard to imagine Him in person, for He was not merely a bird, but a flame as well, and a breath at other times. It may be His light, she thought, which flits at night about the edge of the marshes, His breathing which drives the clouds, His voice which gives harmony to the bells; and she would sit rapt in adoration, enjoying the cool walls and the quiet of the church.

Such was Felicite. Such was my mother. One was a fiction of Flaubert, the other a real woman who gave me birth, who taught me what it means to turn and become like a little child, of whom Heaven is made. Nor did my mother's Franciscan empathy stop with the suffering Jesus or with His mother Mary or with nature around her. It extended in a very literal way to the characters of fiction, as well. She would have identified with Felicite, she would have worried over her as she did over the characters in *The Cardinal*. Mother wrote of that book:

> If I did read *The Cardinal* before, I surely forgot every word. It certainly keeps one reading. Funny-sad and much misery. Starts out as a family. One of the boys, just returned from Rome (a priest). He was serving in one of the churches in his home town. In the meantime the Bishop sent him to a very poor town. People didn't have enough to eat, let alone to help the priests. The church was in pieces. When he rang the bell, I mean knocked at the rectory door, no one came. He walked in. A disaster. Just a piece of rye bread on the table and tea. When the pastor came, he could hardly walk from malnutrition. So the new priest got busy, cleaned up the place, tried to get someone to give them a little money for food. But people would run away from him. There is only 9 or 10 cents in the collection on Sunday. It does get better, though. Right now the pastor is very sick—and only 65.

Stories like this were always real for my mother, from *Huckleberry Finn*, which she read me as a child, to my own, *Francis: The Journey and the Dream*. When she was reading my book on Saint Francis for the first time, she wrote to tell me she didn't know if she would be able to stand seeing him die at the end—he was so good!

I knelt at my mother's side when she died, and the words I wrote of Saint Francis years before became the reality before me, as fiction and reality had been one with her through all her years of loving and empathizing and unifying imagination and reality in her soul the way poets try to bring them together in their poems. She became the dying Francis of *The Journey and the Dream*, so that I had only to change the name from Francis to Polly—the dying was the same:

> Images of Elijah drifted through his mind. He saw the prophet stretched out upon the widow's son, breathing life into the boy. In Francis' mind the two figures of boy and prophet melted into one another. He hoped Jesus' coming to him would be like that. They would melt into one another, limb to limb and wound to wound, and Francis would rise completely in Jesus, flesh of His flesh, and his Journey would be ended and he would be himself. Lost in Jesus, he would still be Francis, but he would also be eternally one with his Divine Lover.
>
> The brothers were all weeping now and praying aloud, but Francis neither saw nor heard. His blind eyes were transfixed, watching the man of the Dream approach him.
>
> "Now, Little One, Sparrow! I am here." And the Lord bent down to Francis. But all that the brothers saw was Francis half rising and leaning forward, his eyes closed, a radiant smile on his face. He seemed to hold a precious gift in his arms. Then he eased back onto the ground and let the lightness of that gift rest upon his heart, and died in the Lord.

Then like the figurines and doilies, the Navajo rugs and drapes mother put into our cedar chests, I put her away, out of the sandstorm's way, into the sweet-smelling earth from which she will rise bright and radiant and free in him she loved to the end.

[1]Philip Larkin, *Collected Poems* (New York: Farrar, Straus & Giroux, 1989), p. 126.

[2]Gerard Manley Hopkins, *Poems and Prose* (New York: Viking Penguin, 1986), p. 27.

[3]John Keats, *Complete Works*.

[4]Zbigniew Herbert, *Selected Poems*, translated by Czeslaw Milosz and Peter Dale Scott, with an introduction by A. Alvarez (New York: The Ecco Press, 1968).

From
Jesus, A Disciple's Search
(1986)

The Story of This Book

Five years ago I was reading the Gospel of John and the following passage leaped from the page, fresh and alive, with a significance it had not had before. As so often happens with the Word of God, I felt something powerful move within me and suddenly Nathanael was very real, a person I somehow recognized.

> The next day Jesus decided to go to Galilee. He found Philip and said to him, "Follow me." Now Philip was from Bethsaida, the city of Andrew and Peter. Philip found Nathanael and said to him, "We have found him about whom Moses in the law and also the prophets wrote, Jesus son of Joseph from Nazareth." Nathanael said to him, "Can anything good come out of Nazareth?" Philip said to him, "Come and see." When Jesus saw Nathanael coming toward him, he said of him: "Here is truly an Israelite in whom there is no deceit!" Nathanael asked him, "Where did you get to know me?" Jesus answered, "I saw you under the fig tree before Philip called you." Nathanael replied, "Rabbi, you are the Son of God! You are the king of Israel!" Jesus answered, "Do you believe because I told you that I saw you under the fig tree? You will see greater things than these." And he said to him, "Very truly I tell you, you will see heaven opened and the angels of God ascending and descending upon the Son of Man." (John 1:43-51)

At that time Jesus seemed removed, absent from my life, and I was trying desperately to find him again, or to do whatever I needed to do for him to find me. I wanted to explore words on the page as a way of being receptive to the Word, but I was afraid of becoming sentimental. I needed a voice to match the voice of my own searching, and that was the voice I heard vibrating in Nathanael's words, "Can anything good come out of Nazareth?"

The skepticism, the implied disappointment, almost disgust, that the Messiah he had longed for so deeply should come from a place like Nazareth, fit well my own disillusioned mood. I found in Nathanael a spirit kindred to my own; I found a tone of voice that I hoped would save my scribblings from sentimentality.

And so I began to write, exploring that voice, knowing at the time very little about Nathanael. I had, in fact, never given him much thought before the writing of these pages. And it was not until I had been writing for some time that I began to wonder about the historical Nathanael and who he might be. Much to my surprise, I discovered that Nathanael is only mentioned in two places in the Bible, the passage above and this one, also from the Gospel of John:

> After these things, Jesus showed himself again to the disciples by the Sea of Tiberias; and he showed himself in this way. Gathered there together were Simon Peter, Thomas called the Twin, Nathanael of Cana in Galilee, the sons of Zebedee, and two others of his disciples. Simon Peter said to them, "I am going fishing." They said to him, "We will go with you." They went out and got into the boat, but that night they caught nothing.
>
> Just after daybreak, Jesus stood on the beach; but the disciples did not know that it was Jesus. Jesus said to them, "Children, you have no fish, have you?" They

answered, "No." He said to them, "Cast the net to the right side of the boat, and you will find some." So they cast it, and now they were not able to haul it in because there were so many fish. That disciple whom Jesus loved said to Peter, "It is the Lord!" When Simon Peter heard that it was the Lord, he put on some clothes, for he was naked, and jumped into the sea. But the other disciples came in the boat, dragging the net full of fish, for they were not far from the land, only about a hundred yards off.

When they had gone ashore, they saw a charcoal fire there, with fish on it, and bread. Jesus said to them, "Bring some of the fish that you have just caught." So Simon Peter went aboard and hauled the net ashore, full of large fish, a hundred fifty-three of them; and though there were so many, the net was not torn. Jesus said to them, "Come and have breakfast." Now none of the disciples dared to ask him, "Who are you?" because they knew it was the Lord. Jesus came and took the bread and gave it to them, and did the same with the fish. This was now the third time that Jesus appeared to the disciples after he was raised from the dead. (John 21:1-14)

How strange that no other evangelist mentions Nathanael. Is he for John only an imaginary construct, a symbol of the true Israelite? Or is he, as some scholars think, the apostle Bartholomew of the other Gospels? Matthew, Mark and Luke never mention Nathanael, and John never mentions Bartholomew. Moreover, in Matthew 10:3 and Mark 3:18, Philip and Bartholomew are mentioned together, as if they are connected in the evangelists' minds. This has led some to believe that Nathanael and Bartholomew are one and the same person, Bartholomew ("son of Tholmai") being his last name, and Nathanael ("gift of God") his first. There is no agreement among scholars, however, and so the true identity of Nathanael remains one of those historical questions that only time and scholarship may one day answer.

But as I wrote, I found myself favoring the opinion that holds they are one and the same person. I remembered the heroic statue of Saint Bartholomew in the Basilica of St. John Lateran in Rome. He is holding his skin over his arm because, according to tradition, he was flayed alive. And I remembered his tomb under the altar of the Franciscan Church of Saint Bartholomew on the Isola Tiberina, the small island in the Tiber near the great Jewish Synagogue of Rome. Nathanael, of Cana in Galilee, began to merge on the page into Bartholomew, the apostle.

Then a couple of coincidences occurred in my reading that encouraged me to continue writing in the voice and person of Nathanael. One was my discovery that Saint Jerome, writing in the fourth century, spoke of a Gospel of Bartholomew consisting of questions Bartholomew puts to Jesus and his mother Mary before the Ascension. This fact helped me to believe it plausible that the Nathanael of my imagination would remember Jesus in the written word. Another refinement of the voice I was discovering came two years later as I was reading *The Divine Comedy* of Dante. At the beginning of the *Paradiso*, the final book of his great poem, Dante calls upon Apollo, god of sun, of light itself:

> Come into my heart, and so breathe
> As you did when you drew Marsyas
> From the skin in which his limbs were enclosed.

Immediately I thought of Saint Bartholomew and how he, too, was drawn from his skin. (The Marsyas to whom Dante refers was a satyr who challenged Apollo to a musical contest. He was defeated and skinned alive for his presumption.) Marsyas became a symbol for me of Saint Bartholomew who, when skinned, reveals the presumptuous Nathanael, who is the metaphor for my own presumptuous questioning.

And so I huddled beneath an imaginary fig tree near the Sea of Galilee, which I have never seen. I became Nathanael beneath his tree, and he became me and all of us who cannot see Jesus but want to so intensely.

All the time I was writing this book I was involved with a psychologically disturbed person whose healing was the most important thing in my life. And that fact has colored the tone of this book, perhaps even more than the voice of Nathanael within me. I could not understand why Jesus did not just come and work a healing. I prayed and prayed and grew disillusioned. I couldn't explain God's failure to act. My own ideas of who God is, of who Jesus is, were trying to force God to do what I wanted. Then, to quote contemporary poet Herbert Lomas, from *Letters in the Dark*:

> As we stand on our dung-heap of ideas and crow,
> He slips away whispering, "I Am," to break bread
> Just when we're discussing his non-existence.

And so in the end, I had only to surrender to his Spirit and let Jesus slip away and then emerge to break bread where he chose, rather than where I wanted. I had to let him come, even from Nazareth.

Prologue

I take as my metaphor, Nathanael:
Nathanael, whose name means "gift of God,"
Nathanael, who might have been the apostle Bartholomew,
or who might have been simply Nathanael,
someone lost in the Bible's pages,
lost in the controversy over his very name.
I become Nathanael in order to remember—
to remember who I am or might become.
But more importantly,
to remember you....

You, Jesus.
Your face in my dreams.
You, standing on the shores of lakes and sides of hills,
your beard ragged and your hair matted
with whatever may have covered the ground
of a night of fitful sleeping.
Your hands rough from the wood of so many years,
your feet caked with dirt and mud,
your clothes dusted with the ever-present sand.

I never forget your eyes upon me,
your eyes and the softness of your mouth,
smiling at all my complexity,
my penchant for strewing confusion
and misunderstanding about me.

How I miss you!
You it was who brought me out,
made it possible for me to believe
I was as good as the others,
to feel my own goodness

rising from within me like Siloe,
a spring of healing water eager to rush outdoors
and spend itself lavishly
on whoever passed my way.

How strange such sentiment sounds,
how unlike me to gush like this about anything.
But that is your power over my powerlessness,
the change you were able to effect in me
because you looked upon me with love,
overlooked what you knew I could not change.

And now I miss you,
because the others, though they love me,
are constantly trying to change me, to make me fit
the icon of who they think we are supposed to be.
And, of course, I do not change
and they grow angry and impatient with me,
and I grow more like I was before.

And so I hope, in this returning,
to somehow reenact what happened
when you walked with us,
standing between me and the others,
a buffer against their disappointment and anger
that I remained stubborn and kept doing things
that made them feel I loved them less than I did.
I never loved them less,
but something perverse in me kept me even from you,
from showing what I have within.

You understood that.
You knew who I was behind my impossible exterior.
But you are no longer here,

and I cannot look into your eyes
and see your acceptance
of who I am,
despite the bitterness that covers my life
like the hard, protective layer of lacquer
you spread over the softness of wood.
And so I remember.

Or try to remember,
for sometimes the memory fades and I cannot see you.
I stop and lean against the mud walls
of an anonymous house I might be passing,
and I feel the fear tightening about my heart
and my pulse pumping wildly
and the dryness of mouth and throat
and the panic that I will slip back to what I was,
that somehow I will lose you.
And I begin to wheeze and wonder:
Is your Spirit trying to leave,
to force his way out of the hollow shell
of what I am afraid I have become?

Sometimes weeks and months pass by
and I cannot find your face,
and then—suddenly, coming around a corner
and meeting a blind or crippled figure
or looking at a slant of light
across a tortured face in the crowd,
I recognize you and reach out to you
and take you in my arms.
And then it begins again,
the criticism and jealousy of those among us
who cannot see your face
in the twisted face I hold in my hands.

They expect it to be made whole
as it so often is for them who pray in your name.

And when it does not happen,
they tell me to leave
and you will make whole without me
what you failed to restore with me.
But I am paralyzed to leave
because I cannot leave you to minister to yourself.
I try to walk away,
but when I turn around to wave,
it is you I see, Lord Jesus,
your eyes upon me,
looking sadly after me walking away from you.
And how can I leave you
who refused to abandon me to the shade
where I sat beneath the tree of my own self-pity?
You refused to give up on who I could become,
on who I already was.
And so I live with all the criticism
and misunderstanding of the others
who love you just as much as I,
but who do not see your face where I see it
because they themselves were never inside
those twisted faces,
as I was.

We find you over and over again, Lord Jesus,
where we ourselves were
when you first found us.
And when we forget to remember
the face we wore when you found us,
then it is that we lose the memory of your countenance.
For your face is our own,

reflected in the faces of those
looking to find your face
in us
whom you have sent as angels,
messengers of the poor God,
whose twisted, tortured body hung
against the evening sky
for all to see what kind of face God wears.

Act I

Morning

1.

You stood here on the shore of the Sea of Galilee,
the wind blowing through your hair
as it blows now through mine.
You saw me under the fig tree in Cana,
far beyond the reach of human eyes.
What you saw is what I have returned to find,
the reason for this strange life
I've lived these past three years.
I have come back to sort out who I was and who I am,
who you were and who you still are.
You, Lord Jesus, the one from Nazareth.

I know who you are now.
I call you Lord.
I did not then, though I said so glibly,
"Rabbi, you are the Son of God! You are the King of Israel!"
And all because you saw me under the fig tree

and flattered me with,
"Well, an Israelite indeed, in whom there is no guile."
I confess your power over me, even then,
your eyes that saw me,
your eyes that saw through me,
saw my heart that day beneath the fateful tree.
Like Adam I met you after the tree,
as I would meet you again three years later
beneath another tree
on that desolate hill of our abandoning you.
You saw me, too, when I hid in Gethsemane in fear,
beneath an olive tree I would have made my gibbet
had I not seen in the distance
the angels ascending and descending upon you.
I whispered, "Son of Man,"
and remembered your words the day I met you.

Again you had seen:

A seeing that led me to that upper room
where the tongues of fire licked my balding head
and penetrated to the secret of the tree
and I knew that I was forgiven, somehow new,
a child again,
guileless
in the way I wanted to be from the beginning.
The way I really was beneath my sarcasm
when I asked, "Can anything good come from Nazareth?"
The way you knew I was all along.

So here I am, back where we began,
waiting for your hand
to lift me up and lead me back to you
that I might understand

how something so good could have come at all.

2.

I sit now beneath a tree
not unlike the tree where you found me.
Ageless branches rich with figs sigh next to me,
and I remember your words.
I am held in their grip,
hating them at times,
at times clinging to them in a way I wish I needn't.
They cast a spell I cannot shake or explain away.
They are who you are now that you are gone.
And you are gone, despite your Spirit.

I suppose your parting is the beginning of faith,
your presence its substitute.
But who am I to try and understand—
I whom you called from the tree of my dreaming,
I who only sat and watched and criticized
the so-called sages
with their convoluted reading of the Law
that turned their eyes inward
until they even looked like men turned inside out?

What is it you said,
"I came to cast fire upon the earth"?
And so you did,
even at your coming as a baby,
a flash of fire upon the straw.
You lit up the cave
from which we all emerge;
you were a flame

that drew people
to the place
where you lay wet and burning
on the manger floor.
And eyes began again to look
outward from the shade of trees,
outward from the tangled brain,
to their Savior, sighted,
focused by a star.

That is what you did for me the day I met you
and heard you call my name:
I began to look outward to you and the One who sent you,
instead of inward to myself.
And even now that we have felt the fire of your Spirit,
my eyes still look outward to the place of your leaving,
to the bright emptiness
your vanishing heels left upon the sky.

I try to lower my eyes
toward those you said were really you
behind the dirt and rags and mouths wagging with hunger;
but the bright space, like your words in my ears,
holds me yet in thrall.
Perhaps this journey backward
will focus my senses again.
I pray it does not end at the tree
where you found me,
my eyes white from staring into the sun
lest they turn and see the darkness within
that looking upon you turned into light.

Act II

Noon

1.

A stooped woman is walking the beach below my tree,
her basket of fish doubling her over with its weight.
She turns almost imperceptibly to where I am sitting.
She eyes me cautiously and walks on, quickly,
her weighted back reminding me of that other woman,
your mother.
Almost as young as you, how old she looked,
how bent, as she held your dead body in her arms
a symbol of the sorrow of all parting.
What can I say now that she is here without you?

Every time I see her and count more gray hairs,
more wrinkles than before,
I wonder who she is,
this fiftyish woman
whose presence plagues us with memories of you.
She reminds me of something feminine in myself,
something I used to fear,
another "I" crying to be heard,
to be placated by something I had to give but would not.
Something vestigial perhaps,
an ending or a prefix to a noun.

Lately, she has begun to walk through my dreams
as if she belongs there,
or is she in fact inside me
because that is where she really dwells, this Mary,
this mother whose presence haunts me

more than your absence,
you who are her only son?
Or are you?

Did I not see my own reflection in your eyes
that day you called me
and every day we walked together?
And yet I never thought
you were the brother I never had,
nor do I now.
Nor is she my mother.
It is something other.

She is somehow me
(I can't believe what I'm saying),
the me you left behind when you ascended to the Father,
taking part of me with you
on the soles of your feet,
the me who is the empty womb you broke through,
rising from death.

Salvation is no longer just an entering in,
but a coming out, as well.
The walls of Jerusalem, the walls of a tomb,
are meaningless now that you have died
and risen beyond them.
From the bosom of your Father
you entered the womb of Mary
in order to come out into the world outside.
In her the walled city took on flesh,
became human, woman;
and all need of mortar and stone became superfluous.
In Mary and through her
all salvation began to happen inside out,

and God kept breaking out
of what was supposed to contain him:
the womb, the tent, the Temple, the city,
even the earth where he lay buried under our sins.
Whatever you entered
became pregnant with your birth
rather than a permanent throne for residing.

All creation is for birthing
rather than enthroning God-become-flesh.
Perhaps that is why your mother moves me so:
In her presence
something in me struggles to conceive.

The mystery of it all staggers me.
Perhaps that is your mother Mary's fascination
for me.
You inhabit her still
and are born again and again through her.
Even now she is like a walking pregnancy,
full of grace, filled with you,
and to touch her
is to touch the mystery
of the enfleshment of God.

I struggle to say it and cannot.
I can only report the ringing in my ears
when she speaks to us.
God is born of woman
is all I can say.
It is so obvious
as to sound like a cliché already;
but it is not grasped,
I am sure,

because we keep looking for you, Jesus,
up there in the heavens.

We keep looking for you in all the wrong places.
(Perhaps I should not even have come here to this lake!)
We remain in Jerusalem,
and you are on the road,
or you are eating supper in some house in Emmaus.

I am spending more time with your mother.
She seems to know where you are.
Or perhaps she carries you to where you should be:
among the poor, the outcast,
the rejected and despised.
She spends little time with us,
as you know,
I'm sure.

2.

And so my memories of you and those around you
are human ones
that only make your divinity more resplendent
for all its human skin.
And Mary leaps into the mind again and again
with all the freshness and color of the mystical bride,
"the eyes behind her veil like doves,
her hair like a flock of goats
streaming down Mount Gilead."

She is all of that and none of that,
because your mother,
when it all started happening,

was merely a poor girl of Nazareth
living the simple, nondescript existence of the poor.
Then there was the angel
and your birth
and the wise men from the East,
the flight into and return from Egypt,
presenting you,
then finding you in the Temple,
and the marriage in Cana, my village,
and the cross and the resurrection.
Those were the extraordinary events,
the events that raised her high above the ordinary.

But it is how she lived
and what she did from day to day that matters,
and it all transpires inside the earthen walls of her home.
She is the divinization of the domestic,
as you are the humanization of the Godhead.
She it was who spoke most truly of you,
she it was who sat quietly
in the shadow of the Temple and spoke with me
and understood my troubled heart
and calmed me with what she remembered
and how she remembered it:

> He rode lightly in my womb like a dream
>   of clouds floating me above the earth
> And I would place my hand on my belly
>   and I would tremble
> At who this would be
>   growing within me, apart from me.
>
> And Joseph, the tender, miraculous man,
>   would place his warm fingertips on the moving Life

And look into my eyes and feel his estrangement
    from what had entered me without him and try
To comfort me when he wanted only to cry.
    And we would sit for hours near the doorway
Where the Sabbath sun made a rectangle box

And plan what we would do when this child,
    whose name we already knew was Jesus,
Would crawl into the sun-box and reach for the light
    with his tiny hand and we would know he was
The Son of God and wonder what he knew—or
    would he
    talk and not be speechless like other children?

And how we cried for joy when he was born
    and did not talk but lay there like a baby and was.
We knew then we need only be like other people until
    the day
when the child became aware of what we already
    knew.

Though he was divine, the Godhead in that tiny body
    revealed itself to him as the Torah reveals itself to a
    rabbi—
Line by line and only when it could be absorbed
    and understood by the student, though this disciple
Knew more but would not know he knew more until
    the dialogue began and the rush of love between
Father and Son took him the way it had taken me
    in his conception.

She leaned back against the Temple wall where we sat—
this woman of fifty or so and I,
who dared to ask and dared as well to listen.

Her feet reached for the spot of sun
that was beginning to inch over the east wall
and she looked at me where I looked on in wonder
at the poetry of her speaking.
She crossed her hands in her lap
and I noticed the small brown spots of age
just beginning to form in a couple of places.

And I wondered if she always talked like this
or if this was one of those special moments for us,
one of those magic moments
when question and answer, speaker and listener
become one
in the spark of encounter that ignites something in the
soul that needs to flame up and burn itself out
that the heart might lie down, tranquil again,
satisfied that its light has shone
before one whose eyes were made to see it.

I dared not speak.
I waited at her feet,
not knowing if the fire was out or not,
not knowing if this was all I would see
of what was kept burning
from all she had stored in her heart like precious fuel.

3.

Though we dared not even think about it,
    we knew we were giving God a home.
And the walls of the house were suddenly mud
    and the floor was dirt and we were poor.
I was pregnant before the seemly time

and our neighbors knew and ostracized us,
And there was much silence at the table
    when Joseph came in from the shop for supper.
We would try to talk about the pleasantries and he
    always smiled and lifted the cup of wine to his lips
Gratefully, as if for the meal and me and everything
    that remained unspoken between us.

But behind the smile, behind the quiet manner,
    I could see the passion and how he wanted to take
        me
In his arms and did not know if he dared with the
    Father of my child still fanning the air about us.
And he would rise and return to the shop after supper
    and I could hear the sawing and the wood falling
And the too heavy clomping back and forth
    as he tried to wear himself out pouring his
Frustrated love into the mechanical movement of arm
    and saw, the methodical stacking of even boards.
And he would then come in after he thought
    I was already asleep and fall exhausted onto the bed
Where I lay, eyes closed and weeping for him.

And then there was the danger from without,
    and we with no means of protection, no hiding
        place
Except in the words we had grown used to hearing,
    words we feared and prayed would not be too hard
In the fulfilling, words that seemed to contradict
    the words of the Law, so that I would lower my eyes
And cling to the wall-side of the street when I was
    out shopping and a rabbi passed by,
Words like those that once startled us in sleep and
    drove us

from our home onto the desert road to Egypt.

And here she lay back and sighed as if the memory were too
    much,
the danger and pain still alarmingly real, even now,
and yet wanting to try to tell it this time,
to exorcise what she never told Joseph or the child
whose safety was responsible for that terrible journey
that was the fulfillment of another prophecy
she would have been happy to have left unfulfilled.

    How I began to resent the Law and the prophets.
        They loomed like monsters in my mind and
           devoured
    Us for their own unalterable purposes. Always
        the Law and the prophets, as if our whole existence
           were
    Only that they might be justified in my son,
        as if he had been born only to make all those
    Unrealized promises come true once and for all, to
        silence
        the scribes and Pharisees whose lives were words.
    Words, and the only way to satisfy them was to
        give them a walking, talking man whose every
    Gesture reminded them of a passage in some
        obscure text so they could beam with discovery.

    Only it did not work that way. The more the words
        came true, the more they felt the young man was
           only
    Using the words to enhance his own ruthless ambition
        to become Messiah and cause dissension and
           overthrow
    The very Law he claimed to be fulfilling and bring

bloodshed upon his people as the Roman heel
crushed
Into the ground the final remnant of our freedom.

And he grew up before my eyes, my very God's Son,
whose own Law lurked in the shadows about the
house,
Like his mortal enemy. And I watched in wonder.
I looked at him and knew who his Father was
And wondered if the boy would ask, and when.
And I began to dread the day he would leave us
In search of his real Father, that inevitable day
that would fulfill the final words and rid us forever
Of the unreasonable demands of the Law become
God.
He would become the Law that thought it was
destroying Him.
But first he had to pass through
those awkward years when a boy tries
To become a man.

And she smiled tenderly
for the first time since her canticle began.

4.

I was about to continue my narrative
when the branches of this tree swayed gently
and I suddenly realized that
the sharp edge is gone from my words;
and I cannot remember when or where it disappeared,
except that the more defined you become in my remembering,
the closer you seem to be

and the more divine is your presence.
I no longer experience the bitterness of your leaving
or feel that skeptical specter rising inside me.
I only want you to be present to me
and help me, as I remember,
to make you present in the words I utter falteringly.
Only you can make my dead words live,
only your spirit rekindles the smoldering fire within them.
My own poor words are becoming the Word.

But there she is again,
her eyes shining with what she is telling me
of how it was with her.

How is it this strange boy, who had clung
    so long to my dress and held my hand to market
And back and through the narrow streets to
    synagogue,
    should now become a man like other boys?
I had thought that with him it would be different,
    that some angel would come in the night
And wing him away while we slept.
    And then he would return one day and stand
In the door fully a man, his eyes deep with prophecy,
    his face still shining from where he had been.

But here he was instead, an awkward boy, his voice
    deepening, a small line of hair sprouting above
His lip, looking at his young mother, wondering if he
    dare ask her what was happening to him.
And I wanting to embrace him and reassure him
    but turning instead to Joseph who saw as well
And took the boy by the hand and walked with him.

They returned, I remember, very late, and
  the boy entered too solemnly, I thought, and
  carefully
As if carrying the burden of a great new knowledge
  that endeared him to me even more and I smiled
As he came to me formally, almost humorously,
  and kissed me protectively upon the forehead.
Joseph winked from where he stood smiling
  at the open door, and I suddenly felt chilled
And saw something frightening flit by the door,
  something that would return for the boy.

  And I reached out and drew my son to myself,
    and he started at the fear I could not hide
  And thought it was because he was beginning
    to grow away from me, and he held me close
  And remembered he was still only a boy.

I could not believe the candor with which she was speaking
and saw that she was tiring
and did not want to remember the rest:
the years of your leaving and Joseph's dying,
the years of rumor and whispered threats upon your life
that became more and more frequent and less quiet
until they were saying openly and boldly
that you were dangerous and must be silenced,
that you blasphemed Yahweh,
that you would surely die
if you continued the madness of your ways.
But she did in fact continue, her head heavy with memories.

  And it did return, the thing in the night,
    and took him away,
  But by that time I was almost relieved.

At last he had found himself
This boy trying to become a man even
    to his thirtieth year.
All his companions were long since
    married with children about the house
And Jesus still came dreamily in from the shop
    and sat down for supper staring vacantly at us
As if expecting some reprimand for being there
    instead of wherever he was supposed to be.
He always seemed so lost, like an abandoned child
    waiting hopelessly for someone to come for him.

And then John began to preach beyond the Jordan
    and Jesus' footsteps began to lighten about the
        house
And a light came into his eyes as if someone was
        finally
    saying something he was interested in.
He asked people about John every chance he got,
    and one day he went to see him and he did not
        return.
And that night I saw the dark thing at the window
    as I lay sleepless in the empty house.

    And, of course, you know the rest, Nathanael.

That was all she ever told me, but it was enough;
and sometimes I still hear her voice
as I am drifting off to sleep
and I see the pain in her eyes and their joy
when she concluded with,
"And, of course, you know the rest, Nathanael."
She had never called me anything but "the Israelite" before,
and I used to imagine you

telling her about the "true Israelite" you had found
sitting beneath a fig tree just as you used to sit
when you did not know who you were
and were feeling sorry for yourself like Jonah.
And she, of course, would remember
because it did in fact remind her of her son
and all the worry she had for what would become of him
who sat in the shade of trees
instead of cutting wood with Joseph.
True Israelites are worthy of the name.
In them God did indeed strive.

5.

"The thing in the night"
that took you away from your mother
was really what most of us call "death,"
that final frustration
of the destiny we have fashioned for ourselves
and which we dared believe was in our grasp.
When you were thirty years old,
you surrendered to the destiny
mapped out for you from all eternity
by the very divinity who was now emerging
from the depths of your own awareness.

You began to yield to that mysterious self
that used to frighten you as a boy,
that voice that held you behind in Jerusalem
when you were twelve,
that self you became before the doctors of the Law
as you sat listening to them and asking them questions
you did not know you knew.

You let yourself be led away
from the familiar, comfortable life you had made for
yourself toward the desert
where, as you said to Peter,
"Another shall gird you,
and lead you where you do not want to go."

All journeys of the spirit begin,
as Abraham's did,
with leaving the comfortable,
familiar land of one's youth
and trekking through the desert of powerlessness;
and they all end with words like yours on the cross:
"Father, into your hands I commit my spirit."
And as I sat talking to Mary
in the shadow of the Temple,
I suddenly realized
that your journey
had been a journey from your mother to your Father.
The great and terrible chasm that opened beneath you
could only be bridged by letting go of your mother's hand
and somehow leaping far enough
toward your Father's outstretched hand
to catch it and not fall into the void.

That is what you meant by faith, isn't it?
The journey from mother to Father
across the void
that letting go of a mother's hand created.
Now I understand
your mother's willingness to let you go
and how she smiled
when she spoke of you not returning
to the house of your youth.

She realized, didn't she,
that you had finally met the angel she met as a young
girl and that you were letting go of her
as she had of her parents, Joachim and Anne;
that your failure to return
meant you had heard your Father's voice
and had accepted your manhood
as she had her womanhood
when she said,
"Behold the handmaid of the Lord;
let it be unto me according to your word"?

And Mary was then at peace because she knew
that in embracing your manhood,
you discovered what she had known from the beginning
and dared not say:
"You are God's beloved Son; in you he is well pleased."

Act III

Night

1.

There are no fires burning by the sea this evening.
There is only my heart burning as I sit by this lake,
a solitary soul searching the shore for other souls
emerging from the evening mist.
From time to time someone does,
but at a distance,
and my solitude is undisturbed,
my monologue with you uninterrupted.

These moments, inside,
days and nights by the sea,
prepare a place in me
for moving inland when morning comes
and the sun burns off the fog,
and I face again the daily search for you
in the lives who pass by
the indifferent shore of my praying.

Soon I will leave you by the remembered sea
where I have seen you cooking fish
for me to eat at nightfall.
And I will leave and return
to find you there, or not,
depending on whom I bring with me.

You, Lord of the sea,
Lord by the sea,
you are the God of the border
between land and water,
between the sky and the land and the sea.
And your small human fire
lights the place where all the elements meet
in the human God who waits for us
to come from the sea or the land
to sit by the fire and eat the fish you cook,
the fish you are become.
And we lay all our daily selves upon the fire
to be consumed by all who eat with you,
by all whose food is the human God
who sits and waits
where earth and water endlessly embrace,
warming the air with their fire.

Mist touches me as I talk with you,
a dense cover from which no man or woman,
no bird or animal has emerged,
an insulating fog
keeping you here a little longer.
A time for dreaming.

I close my eyes,
and there is Peter working furiously with his nets
lest he lose a minute of fishing
should the fog lift and it be a clear night.
And John is there hoping the fog will stay,
and all we other apostles and followers
are somewhere in between.

But whether I go or stay, come night,
it is you who holds me or sends me,
keeps me by the shore or draws me back
to the small fire and the fish.
All movement to and from
revolves about this place by the sea.
The center is you
cooking fish by the Sea of Galilee
whose water caresses the shore of my human heart.

2.

I look up and
the moon is a small wafer in the sky
above my right shoulder.
There is so little time now
before I return to the world outside
and leave you where you found me

by the ashes of the fire
where I began my journey.
Now there is no safeness of sun,
and darkness brings me
to my knees
as it has every night
since your leaving.
In my grief, I cannot seem
to keep my thoughts from turning
to your suffering and death,
the flames rising higher,
consuming the fish,
leaving only the ashes
that you fanned into flame again
as you rose from their cold,
extinguished center.

And again it is your mother I turn to.
Knowing that you would die very soon,
what did she do,
this Mary, the woman whose face haunts me
in my own night of grief?
I see her as I left her,
sitting there upon the ground,
the Temple weighing down her shoulders,
and she like a bundle of discarded clothes
thrown against the walls, the foundations of Israel.
What did she do when she knew
you would die,
you, her lovely son?
How did she get over losing you,
and how can I?

I ask that question many times, Lord Jesus,

especially when I realize how helpless we are
to stave off death
and someone close to us is dying
and we are supposed to have a faith
that moves mountains
because we are your disciples.
Discipleship does not seem to make it any easier,
except that I do have you to call upon,
and vent my anger on, and cry to in my sorrow.

I think of your mother watching you die,
and you become every human pair.
You become every loved one who has died
and she the one who is helpless, watching it all happen,
she believing only that she too will die
of worry and then of grief.

Confronted with death,
we want to kill whatever insults us
with the deception that this corpse before us
is really alive in some other world.
Was it in fact your promise to rise again in three days
that made us kill you?
Who knows?
And surely it made no difference to your mother
what the reason was.
She only knew you were moving headlong into death;
she saw you dying from living too intensely.
And there was nothing she could do,
except try to remember all that had happened,
especially those portentous events that preceded your birth,
except try to search the Scriptures for some hope
that you would be saved in the nick of time.

And perhaps like me she turned to Isaiah,
who had spoken so glowingly of your birth,
hoping he would reveal the meaning of your death.
Or did she look to you, her son,
for the answer to what would become of us all?
I can't know, of course,
but even if she did and found there an answer,
it did not prevent her
from suffering death vicariously with you
before she arrived at some resolution.

As she stood helplessly
beneath your cross and watched you die,
Mary became every one of us in the face of what is human,
what is mortal and beloved.
She watched her own flesh dying in you.

3.

And so I return to the question I began with.
What did she do, your mother,
when she saw you were going to die
and like us was helpless to prevent it?
What did she do then
she who had said in your conceiving,
"Behold the handmaid of the Lord;
be it done to me according to your will"?
What she cannot change
she brings inside her heart and makes it her will.
And that is what she did
when she knew you were going to die a violent death
like so many of the prophets before you.

Mary knew she could not save you from death
because in some mysterious way
it was death itself that would save you,
and through that very death
she who wanted to save you would herself be saved.
She had heard you say,
"Unless the grain of wheat fall into the ground and die,
it will not live."
And she understood.

Unfortunately, however,
understanding and acceptance do not take away the pain
of watching and waiting
for the inevitable death of someone we love.
It only heightens the pain
because we know what we wish we didn't know.
And we cannot think about it
and grieve over it all the time,
and so we continue the routine of our lives,
our domestic chores,
even our joking and trying to relax
and caring for our health,
as if we are to live forever.

And the days pass and we toss fitfully in bed
and wake to the nightmare of the other's death.
We rise earlier and fall asleep
more from exhaustion than relaxation.
And that perhaps is how it was with her who knew,
before we did,
what cup would be offered you in Gethsemane
and what you would say,
that echo of her own words to the angel so many years before:
"Only not as I will but as you will, Father."

And so Mary becomes who we all are at the core,
mortal beings trying to hold back death
until we can accustom ourselves to its frightening visage
in the slow decay or swift passing of those we love.
She had to reach deep down inside,
where you said the Kingdom is
and try to find there
some way of coping with death,
some strength, some hope beyond the grave,
anything to heal the wide wound of separation.

And what she found,
I like to think,
is your own words to Martha that fateful day
you rose with her brother, Lazarus, from the dead:
"I am the resurrection and I am life;
if you believe in me, even though you die,
you shall come to life;
and no one who has life, and has faith in me
shall ever die."
And she knew that the sword that would pierce her own
soul would be the sword that pierced your side
from which flowed the life
by which we all would live forever.

But then, could she live on words?
Was she, like Abraham and so many holy ones before her,
the kind of person who could live
on the promise of things to be fulfilled?
She had to be,
or she never would have consented
to be your mother in the first place.
And now this waiting for your death
was like waiting for you to be born,

or, at Nazareth all those years,
for you to begin the ministry of dying
by which we were to live.
Who can say which waiting was the hardest for her
and which was more like death?

It is perhaps the waiting itself that is the hardest,
and all the uncertainty and anxiety
over what we will do and how we will respond
to the surprises of Yahweh
that is the real dying.
Surely she had died with you many times before,
as on the flight into Egypt
and when she thought you were irretrievably lost
on that journey to Jerusalem when you were twelve.
Perhaps those and all the other dyings
made it easier for her
to handle your approaching death.

But most probably it did not.
For what we know and what we have already experienced
is never sufficient to remove the sting
when we hold in our arms
the broken body of our own child
who should be holding us in death.

That was the sword in Mary's heart,
and that moment of your lying lifeless in her arms
revealed the deepest pain of the human heart.
And the pain was not diminished
simply because you rose from the grave
three days later.
The future was not yet.
We suffer the present,

and it is not changed to joy
until a future hope becomes the present reality.

So now like Mary we live on the promise
that in you the present pain is not forever.
It changes into joy
when your future becomes our present.
For the future has been transformed
into an eternal present
by your dwelling there with the Father
waiting to be made complete
in our joining you.
We will live forever.
But the way there is still death
and that has not changed.
It is the painful sword
that reveals the thoughts of many hearts.

Like Mary we still have to hold death in our lap
and embrace it if we are to live forever.
But knowing that does not make the cold body warmer,
the broken body whole,
the heavy weight light like pious thoughts.
For then it would not be dead
and we would not know how heavy life is
before it takes wings.

Act IV

Dawn

1.

It is morning.
I have finally slept.
A few hours at most,
and then only from exhaustion.
Too much thinking,
too much in the head for my own good.

There is a chill in the air
and there is no sun.
Only clouds hiding
what we call the sky,
that blue eternity above.
Or are the clouds also sky,
and we have made the heavens sky
only when they are blue?

Here beneath the tree of my sleeping,
sweet with scent of fig,
the gray above is all the sky there is,
and it contents me somehow
that I can call it sky
and not wait for the clouds to pass
and the sun to shine and the color blue to reappear.

Suddenly I realize that is how it is with you and me,
Lord Jesus.
I do not wait for you to return
for you to be the risen Lord;

you already have,
behind the gray that hides you from our sight.
Your name is Savior Lord,
no matter what the color of your appearing.
It is who you are
and what you did that make you Lord,
not the radiance of your countenance shining
clear and unmistakable
like sun on a blue and cloudless day.
You are Lord,
in hiding or in revealing
who you are,
as on that evening you sat down to a meal again
in the startled home at Emmaus.

You were the risen Lord
even before you revealed yourself at supper,
even as you had walked the road earlier that day,
conversing and asking questions like some stranger
to all the events of your own life.
And they did not recognize you,
those two pilgrims walking the road to find you,
and so they told you about yourself,
"a prophet mighty in deed and word
before God and all the people,
and our chief priests and rulers
delivered him up to be condemned
and crucified him.
But we had hoped
that he was the one to redeem Israel.
Yes, and besides all this,
it is now the third day since this happened.
Moreover, some women of our company amazed us.
They were at the tomb early in the morning

and did not find his body;
and they came back saying
that they had even seen a vision of angels,
who said that he was alive.
Some of those who were with us
went to the tomb,
and found it just as the women had said;
but him they did not see."

And then you opened up for them
the gray sky that was always sky
though they called it clouds;
you began with Moses and the prophets
and opened up in the Scriptures
everything that was really about you
though you lay hidden behind the clouds
we did not know were sky.

I don't know how it can be said
except paradoxically:
What we see as sky or cloud is
what we have previously chosen to name it.

2.

You walked to Calvary,
the place of the skull
just outside Jerusalem's wall,
and I turned away,
returning in memory
to the tree of our meeting,
hoping to find its rhythm again,
the contour of its movement against the sky,

the strength of its roots in the earth.
And there I sat, paralyzed against its trunk,
waiting for something to happen without me,
waiting for you to come and find me again.

Something drove me inside
to the tree's image,
some inner compulsion that said
I had to realign myself with a movement
deep inside trees,
that said surrendering to their roots and trunks and
branches would enable you to find me when you came again.
Everything seemed out of joint,
and I knew that nothing we could do
would bring things back into place again.
We, like everything else that lives,
had somehow to find our inner movement once more.

I did not know it then, but in that movement
we would find you
as you rose from the dead,
through the deep roots of the tree
that held your lifeless body
high against the darkened sky.
You would rise in us
as if from some invisible root
that reaches down through our bodies
into the Garden we were banished from
when Yahweh found us standing beside another tree,
ashamed of our nakedness.

And so I sat and dreamed
the fig tree night and day,
until the morning of your rising

when we were all called together
to wait in the upper room.
I remember thinking that
we should be waiting by some tree.
The room, of course, was better
for your return
for that is where you said good-bye
to those of us gathered to eat
the Paschal meal.
You would find us again as *Church*
in the breaking of the bread;
you would find us as *individuals* beneath the tree
of our abandoning you.

So I sat beneath the tree
waiting for you to return and take away
the shame of my soul, naked before you.
You had done it before,
three days of years ago.
You would do it again
as I descended with you into the earth
toward that Paradise whose geography
is the human heart redeemed.

3.

In hiding I watched you
walk heavily to Calvary.
Now I watch you walk through doors
though you appear as substantial
as when you walked lightly upon the water
though you weighed, I'm sure,
as much as I do now.

Is your risen body the same body as mine
which now aches against this tree?
The same body, light though heavy,
and heavy with presence,
yet able to slip between the grains of wood
into the room where Thomas the Dullard
places his hand into your side
and feels the flesh parting
and the slick blood upon his fingertips?
If your hand now
is the same hand that beckoned me,
then everything we have believed is true,
and we are made whole
in your resurrection from the dead.

It must be so,
for we are without imagination
to dream so perfect a dream
of who you have become in saving us,
death revealing your immortality,
as you promised it would,
though all of us forgot what you said
almost as soon as the words passed your lips.
In your glorified body we are made whole,
brought together so perfectly
that we can pass freely through all of creation
as you have passed through the closed doors
separating us from creation.
And without you we live eternally fragmented,
forever disintegrating,
our whole being an exploding universe,
experiencing for all eternity
its being pulled asunder.
To die apart from you

is to be pulled apart from ourselves
and from all of creation contained within us.
And the tension between the fragments
and the center that cannot hold them
is what you meant by sin that leads to real death.

How extraordinary this passage of yours
through doors you used to make in that Nazareth workshop!
Is this then the real craft you were learning there,
the penetration of, the passage through?
Is this what moved you to state so grandly once,
"The Son cannot do anything at his own pleasure.
He can only do what he sees his Father doing;
what the Father does is what the Son does in his turn"?
Though I see it only vaguely, I think it was.

What is solid,
what is worked by human hands,
is somehow penetrable by the human person
raised to life in you and through you.
And now your Spirit has penetrated even my tough skull
so that I am thinking thoughts like these,
not knowing how I am thinking them.
And yet how relieved I am
that I can still think at all,
after what happened in Jerusalem
on that wood I thought to be impenetrable.
But hanging there, I now see,
gave you the passageway through
the very wood that killed you.

Wood, always wood with you,
from that stable you were born in,
to the shavings on the floor

where you worked as a boy into manhood,
to the boat you preached from,
to the tree you found me under,
to the tables you overturned in the Temple
and later ate from at the Passover meal,
to the crossed beams you carried to Calvary,
to the doors from which you emerged
into the room where everyone shivered
behind the wood that reminded them
of the narrow door to Paradise.
Little did we know when you were with us
how narrow that door really is
and what must happen to us
before we can slip between the grains of wood
into the glory of emergence.

4.

What we knew at first
was only what was *not* there in the tomb.
Your body was nowhere to be found.
The women who went to the tomb
to anoint your body with spices and ointments
said they found the stone rolled away
and, when they entered it,
they could not find your body.
And then two angels appeared to them
as men in dazzling clothes and said,
"Why do you seek the living among the dead?
Remember how he told you, while he was still in Galilee,
that the Son of Man must be delivered
into the hands of sinful men and be crucified,
and on the third day rise."

My reaction to the women's report
was typical of me then.
I remarked how fitting it was
that now we were supposed to believe,
purely on negative testimony,
that you had risen from the dead.
Once again God is present by his absence,
by what we don't see,
by what is not there.
The whole scenario fit my skepticism perfectly.
From the beginning
we were asked to believe in things we couldn't see or hear,
in a God who was a Spirit like the wind
which blew where it would and was known
only as it passed invisibly among us.

Or we were expected to believe
that you were the Messiah,
the Son of God,
though we saw so much humanness in you.
Always the same,
faith resting on what was not there,
not seen,
while what was seen and heard
proclaimed the opposite
of what we were supposed to believe.
How I longed for some confirmation
that what had happened three years before,
beneath the tree of my becoming,
was in fact what I thought it was
and not some mere coincidence.

What had happened to you and among us
from the hour of your betrayal by Judas

to the moment of the women announcing
that the tomb was empty of your body
was too great a trial of our faith
to be reversed by the negative testimony
of the women who loved you.
After all, the authorities had every reason
to remove your body by night,
lest your tomb become the shrine
and rallying point of the stories
they sought to discredit.
Besides, our sorely tested souls
would never base our belief
that you had risen from the dead on our inability
to find the body that Joseph of Arimathea
claimed to have removed from the cross,
wrapped in a linen shroud,
and laid in a rock-hewn tomb
without the proper anointing
because it was the Day of Preparation,
and the Sabbath was beginning.

And that is why I have now risen
from the day and night of this tree
and walked down to the shore of the lake
where we saw you on the shore as alive and human
as when we walked the same shore together
and you were fit and well,
robust in your young manhood,
eager for sharing Yahweh's word.
A word you never wrote down
lest it become Law like Moses' words to us;
A Word you kept living out in your person,
forcing us to keep our eyes on you,
knowing that it was you who had to convince us,

not what you had to say.
You were the Word.

We believed it then;
we know it now that we have seen you
walking upon the shore.
And everything the Word became in you
came together as you knelt upon the rocky shore
and built a fire and cooked the fish
and gave it to us to eat with bread.
You did upon the ground by the Sea of Galilee
what you did upon the hill of Calvary.
And we understood what you were doing
and knew we would do the same
whenever we met to eat the meal
and drink the wine consumed
in memory of you.

You were really writing the Word in the earth
where it belongs, as you had done before,
that day they brought to you the woman caught in adultery
for you to pronounce your Father's word of judgment
and you surprised us all by writing it in the dirt
where alone it can be found.
And now, Lord Jesus, you reconfirm on the ground by the sea
what happened on the bare ground of Bethlehem,
what was consummated as your blood fell
upon the soil of Calvary,
and what rose out of the dark ground that Sunday
the women went looking for you in the earth.

5.

Jesus by the sea,
you blow upon the embers of a little seaside fire
and the flame is rekindled,
and your breath moves over the land
onto the dark water
where we bob up and down watching our nets:
Simon Peter and Thomas "the Twin,"
the sons of Zebedee and two other disciples,
and I who now stand here alone
trying to remember how it was.

It comes back to me clearly,
as if everything that is illumined
by your bright presence on the beach
that has become these words,
becoming now
my own canticle:

        You sit by the sea,
        small fire and one fish
        and no clouds
        aflame with angels.
        You wait for us
        to row toward you
        your human hand
        stirring embers.

        And you're revealed again
        when we partake of food,
        the skeleton of whose name
        becomes your signature.
        The fisherman is at last the fish

and we the fishers of God.

6.

A place of land and water and you
and the wind, always the wind blowing.
That is where we left you standing,
once more sending us away from the sea and our boats
moored where the water meets the land.
We had thought that it was over
and knew nothing of what to do,
except return to boats and water.

"I am going fishing," Peter said,
and we went with him down to the Sea of Galilee
and caught nothing that night
and it seemed like those former times of boredom
when fishing was all there was
and my only refuge was daydreaming
and withdrawal into my own mind.
No one said as much,
but we were acting
as though the past three years
were but an interlude,
a fisherman's brief adventure on land,
something to remember on long nights
and longer days
as we sat watching the net-floats bob,
mesmerizing strained eyes.

We were back to who we used to be,
and we did not really expect
that you would once again stand on the shore

and ask us to follow you and send us forth.
But you did,
and this time it was even more mysterious than the first;
for as you sent us inland again,
we turned to wave
and you suddenly dissolved into sea-mist
where you stood,
and we saw nothing but boats and water
and the smoldering fire you had built upon the sand.

7.

Tree-roots in the sand.
Wind and water meeting trees and land.
The memory never fades.
There is only your bright presence
emerging from and dissolving into sea-mist,
your bright feet ascending from Mount Olivet into the cloud,
only your bright Spirit returning
with the sound of a mighty wind,
filling the house where we are sitting.
And there appear to us tongues as of fire,
and they rest upon each one of us,
and we are filled with your Holy Spirit.
And we become the wind in which you move
through the branches of the trees,
over land and water,
making all thing new.
And I,
even I,
am the stuff of wind and fire.

Epilogue

And so I leave you, Nathanael,
in your marble sarcophagus
beneath the altar of your church
on this island in the Tiber.
In a final irony
even your name has been erased
and you have become a perhaps-apostle.
Nathanael, found beneath a fig tree in Galilee,
now you are Bartholomew,
skinned, floating in the Tiber
between Trastevere and the great Jewish synagogue of Rome.

I have knelt this morning at your tomb
(wondering if it is your tomb)
to take my leave,
to ask your intercession: that
through you, Saint Bartholomew,
I might somehow find my way back
to the tree of Nathanael,
and know the journey you made
from Galilee to Rome and back again
to the tree near the shore of the sea.

St. Bartholomew's Church
Rome, Isola Tiberina